LOSING A SPOUSE

Anna Ingolfs and Gudfinna Eydal

LOSING A SPOUSE

On love, grief and recovery

Real books © 2014

To our husbands Árni Margeirsson and Egill Egilsson

Special thanks to Ellie Kaastra and to our editor Christopher Noël

Losing a spouse
ISBN 978-9935-9185-0-5

Cover Design:
Gunnar R. Kristinsson

Typeset in Iceland by:
Imyndunarafl – design studio

TABLE OF CONTENTS

FOREWORD BY GUDFINNA

Writing this book has been a unique experience for me, both as a psychologist and as a person. Working on the book might be described as a certain kind of therapy that has helped me a great deal.

Because of how close this project is to my heart and how important it has been to me, I would like to take this opportunity to say a few words about myself, particularly about my relationship with Egill, my husband of 42 years. I have now been given an opportunity to see with even greater clarity what a good and beautiful relationship we had. I also wish to pay my thanks to life for the great fortune of meeting just this man.

Over the years I sometimes said to Egill that when the time came for one of us to die and leave the other, I would rather be the one to leave first. He understood what I meant. He knew that because of a certain separation I experienced as a child, it was extremely difficult for me to be rejected or left behind. But now as I write this and have begun to recover from my grief, I am relieved that he should have been the first to go, for I believe that his grief would have been heavy and of long duration.

He sometimes joked with me and others and said mischievously that my next book would be entitled "The Years with Egill". Then he laughed out loud. For this very reason, I would like to put together a few words about our life, love, and marriage. In spite of being a specialist in clinical psychology and knowledgeable about trauma and responses to trauma, I experienced grief in full force and am still dealing with it in some ways. Yet my knowledge helped me to admit how I felt and that I would have to be tenacious. My understanding of grief told me that my reactions were natural and that the only way to survive and go on was to go through the pain.

MY YEARS WITH EGILL

I saw you for the first time in late August of 1966 at the main dance club in my North Icelandic hometown of Akureyri, which at the time was the second-largest town in the country. I had just graduated from secondary school and was heading to the capital, Reykjavík, to earn some money so I could go abroad to study psychology. I wanted to go to Aarhus in Denmark, whose university had a good reputation in the field. I can't remember anymore why I did go to this dance. I went alone and had no plans to meet anyone in particular, as most of my friends were away. Perhaps it was to see my cousins, who were popular throughout the country as musicians. They were playing that night, and I loved their music. I was dressed up and had teased my hair, as was the fashion back then when going out. I was pretty pleased with myself as I walked up the stairs of the club and headed straight for the bar to get a Moscow Mule (vodka and ginger ale). I will never forget the first time I saw you, standing there at the bar, tall, tan, with short hair and a muscular physique. Your hair was reddish and cropped close, and you wore a light-colored suit. You were handsome, and I thought you stood out from the crowd. You noticed me as soon as I approached, and as we looked straight into each other's eyes for a moment, something happened. We both felt it. I sat down by the bar with my drink, and after a few moments you came and asked me to dance. We danced together all night, including the slow dance at the end. Your name was Egill and you told me you had just returned from a month's travels around the entire United States. You had been visiting a favorite cousin who worked there as an engineer. It made sense now how tanned and handsome you looked – most redheads just turned pink after catching the sun in Iceland. You were four years my senior and had lived in Copenhagen for three years, studying physics. You were halfway through your studies but had been asked to come home to teach physics for a year, as you had been a model student. You didn't feel you could deny your old schoolmaster's request, even though you were loath to interrupt your university studies. You reminded me of someone I couldn't quite place, and I told you as much. With your famous sense of humor and the twinkle in your eye that I'd come to know so well, you said, "That wouldn't be President Kennedy, by any chance?" As a matter of fact, that fit the bill. The explanation proved to be that while you traveled in the States, children would call out to you, "You look like President Kennedy." You couldn't see the resemblance yourself, but I knew exactly what they meant. Handsome, with an attractive boyish air, a warm and beautiful smile and a confident demeanor.

After that memorable evening, I went on to Reykjavík, and you, who were three hundred miles away, said you would visit me in October. I was rather insecure but very excited for the intervening month. Would the man come, or was this just a pleasant autumn interlude we had shared in the town where we had both grown up? Of course you kept your promise. You kept every promise you made, were one hundred percent reliable. We met yet again at a dance club in Reykjavík, and from that time onward we were inseparable. We spent that Christmas together and remained in close contact all winter. In the autumn of 1967 we went together to Copenhagen, where I enrolled in the University of Copenhagen as a psychology student. At Christmas that year we were married in the beautiful church at Akureyri and were husband and wife for forty-two years.

THE COPENHAGEN YEARS

We spent nine years in Copenhagen together. These were years of great growth and maturing, not least for me, who was young and living abroad for the first time. My studies were challenging and you were halfway done with your physics degree. These were happy years. There was plenty going on for young people, the '68 generation kept life interesting, and we were certainly a part of that. The Psychology Department at the University of Copenhagen was famous for when the students took over the department with the slogan "Out with the professoriate!" We participated in protest marches, had lots of fun, and made our best Danish and Icelandic friends. Drank beer and listened to lots of music. Bob Dylan, the Beatles and the Rolling Stones were the best, apart from high classical music. You grew your hair out and attended a party in a dress on one occasion, and I gave you a run for your money with my long hair done up in the back and colorful clothing. We often stayed up late and discussed things deeply, debating politics and social issues down to the last detail. We wanted to make a difference and fight for justice in the world; nothing with human interest was irrelevant to us. Looking back, it has a comical tinge to it, but this is life, and young people's enthusiasm, eagerness, and camaraderie is a wonderful thing.

During these years, you were wiser and more mature than me, as well as much more self-confident, and I learned infinitely much from you. You gave me great strength in these years by encouraging me personally and in my studies. I was a klutz in the natural sciences, and your unstinting support proved invaluable for my studies. You were also philosophically inclined and thought a great deal about existential questions. Though you were an atheist and I had a more ambivalent take on those matters, we were able to connect well in conversation. You were a rational scientist, but without prejudice and always prepared to examine every side of a topic. One thing we always agreed on was that in nature, at least, God is manifest.

You were like a rock for me whenever anything went wrong. When I had a personal crisis as a student, a reckoning with my parents and childhood and a profound inner struggle attendant to that, you were my greatest source of help, though I received good professional assistance as well. You supported me, showed me understanding, and helped me to find the right external sources of help. Your advice at this time was invaluable to me, and I am eternally grateful for having experienced the depth of your empathy and your sincere and unconditional love. You really can't ask for more from another human being.

There was little conflict between us. We agreed so well on most things. Our tastes in everything from people to furniture were similar. Both of us had a good sense of humor, laughed a lot and made merry, though our temperaments were quite different. You were far more changeable than me and could lose your temper, but you were just as quick to regain equilibrium. I was more even-keeled, but more prone to hold a grudge and could be stubborn. This combination worked well and didn't cause us to lock horns too much, though we had our disagreements. We always discussed things, and neither of us liked to be at loggerheads for long. We never used silence or froze each other out, and neither of us wanted loud and aggressive fights, though we might come into conflict on rare occasions.

It wasn't easy to move back to Iceland from Denmark after nine years for me and thirteen for you. Bidding all our Danish friends goodbye was a major watershed, and I felt that an era was ending before I was quite ready to part ways. As I write this now, all our best friends in Denmark have passed away. They all died too soon, like you yourself when you departed. I often find it quite unreal to think of all these people who are gone. For a long time I felt like this was some kind of nonsense, and sometimes I've also wondered whether I'm not dead, too. The feeling that enveloped me after losing so many dear friends in less than ten years was an inexplicable combination of grief, awareness, and lack of awareness about life. It was also a positive feeling toward being alive, a sense of gratitude for that. I also felt I had an inner realization that death is a fact, and that it is no longer strange to me. Death just comes when it wishes, and I know that now. I have fully internalized that knowledge. You slowly begin to understand that death is a part of life, something that maybe doesn't dawn on people until they meet death again and again. That's just the way it is, and no one can change that. I had more desire to go back to Iceland than you. I found that strange then, as you loved Icelandic nature more than anything else in the world. Didn't you long to go home to the mountains and waterfalls, the pure air and clean water? I couldn't be without all that. So strong are the ties that bind. I began to understand it better, all this about roots and how deep they run. I knew that despite Denmark and Iceland's both being part of Scandinavia, one was still a foreigner in any other country but one's own and would never adapt completely.

You never regretted going home and thanked me often for it, though life was far more difficult here than in Copenhagen and your professional opportunities in Iceland much more limited.

THE ICELAND YEARS

Our years in Iceland were when everything was happening in our lives. We purchased a house, and established ourselves professionally. We had three children, a daughter born in Denmark and identical twin boys. In these years, when the children needed constant care and attention, we had to rely completely on each other. Otherwise we would have been unable to shoulder our personal and professional responsibilities and take good care of our family and external affairs. Your parents had both passed away, mine lived over three hundred miles away, and all of our friends and acquaintances were busy themselves. We relied on daycare providers to help us take care of the children. It all worked out somehow, but these years tested to the limit what a good couple we were, a good team, able to work with each other like one person and support each other. I've often thought of families where three children are born in four years, including a set of twins. This requires not just endurance but great solidarity, in addition to which a heavy dose of good humor and joy in being entrusted with such a task is never amiss. When I meet the parents of twins on the street, I always give them a smile. These parents the world over have all my admiration and empathy. It was completely strange to us to have twins. We hardly knew any, had none in the family, and had never entertained the possibility that we might have twins ourselves. But life is unpredictable, not only when it comes to losing someone, but also when new life is created. Thank goodness we don't know in advance what awaits us. It would be dreadful if we had to try to prepare ourselves for this and that event that was written in our future. Where would courage and tenacity be then? My first response to the news that we were expecting twins was to say, "I'm not sure whether I am happy about this," and as soon as the doctor had finished his sentence, you chimed in with "How are they going to fit in the car?" We obviously replicated typical feminine and masculine reactions when something unexpected happened and we had no time to prepare our responses.

The first year with three small children was an incredible experience. We just had to survive day by day. Sleepless night after sleepless night; one of the boys fell ill, had to be hospitalized and later underwent surgery; I breastfed every three hours to the point where the feedings blurred into one continuous memory. We were often at our wit's end, and our eldest child got far less than her fair share of attention for a time. Once in the middle of the night, as we sat and fed the boys from bottles, you fell asleep sitting in the chair with the child in your arms, while I ran to the bathroom to throw up, still holding the other boy. The following day you were unable to go to work, and this was the only day you took off in the wake of the birth.

The years after the infant phase was over were busy. We often had fun together and time passed quickly. The children were no longer sick as often, and everything went pretty well, though we had plenty to do. We had many wonderful moments with our children, but also the two of us alone together, as we tried to make sure to do things we enjoyed together to bolster our relationship as a couple. We always loved spending time together, it was usually the best thing in the world. Apart from your work as a physicist, you wrote novels, and our conversations related to your books were very rewarding.

We traveled a great deal, both at home and abroad, and our children usually came along. Scandinavia, Spain, Greece, London, and Glasgow, but the Greek Isles were a special favorite. Once, the family went to Florida for Christmas, and that was quite an experience. We were healthy, vigorous, and active, and enjoyed being a family and having each other. We were happy and felt blessed with good fortune in life.

When you were about forty-three years old, you woke up in the middle of the night once and said, "I think I'm dying, I can't feel my heart beating. Call an ambulance." As you were carried down the stairs on the stretcher and the children and I watched you in a state of utter shock, the thought flew through my mind that you might die and leave us. As you lay there on the stretcher, I said, "How am I supposed to pay the mortgage?" You often laughed at this and sometimes brought this story up at parties, saying, "What do you think my wife said when I was taken to the hospital, possibly at death's door?" But as you did, you cast a warm look and your kindest smile my way. Who could have understood my worries better than you? Later on, I often pondered how an emotional being like myself could become so preoccupied with practical details at critical moments. We can surprise ourselves so much with our unprepared reactions to the unexpected.

It turned out that you had cardiac arrhythmia and they "only" needed to restart your heart. The doctors said this wasn't dangerous but might reoccur from time to time, which it did now and then over the years. The next bout occurred when we were on holiday in Italy and the plan was to enjoy life for a week without children. That stay ended with you in hospital, and I won't forget it any time soon. We didn't worry too much about the arrhythmia, though, because the doctors always insisted that there was nothing to fear. You got a pacemaker in 2007, which was considered wise, but still we were told your condition wasn't dangerous. I remain convinced that this arrhythmia played some part in your sudden cardiac arrest and death two years later, despite the doctors' protestations.

It was a major decision in our life when we built a summer house in one of the most beautiful parts of Iceland. Situated high up in the hills, it had a view over glaciers, the volcano Hekla, rivers, and waterfalls. A true gem, sheer Paradise. This place enabled us to become almost one with nature. Here was our God, here we wished to live and die. You nearly had your wish granted, as your body rests in earth by the little country church about two and a half miles from the summer house, where a grave by your side awaits me.

The time we spent together at the summer house was filled with mindfulness, a sort of spiritual honeymoon in our lives. Nature's magic brought us even closer and encouraged us to express beautiful thoughts to each other. You often said to me, "You are my life," and I told you how grateful I was to have met you. After your death, I was unspeakably grateful that a few days earlier, I had been gripped with the need to tell you in detail why you meant so much to me. I was just compelled to express this thought, right at that very moment. A prominent thought in my mind as I grieved you was that I had been unable to say goodbye to you before you passed away. It was a certain consolation that I'd had this chance to tell you how important you were to me.

THE END OF OUR YEARS

We sat in the hot tub early in the morning of December 12th, 2009. It was near dark outside, but the weather was good, with temperatures of about 48°F (9°C). That's quite warm for this time of year in Iceland. We talked about how maybe there wouldn't be any winter. Patches of green grass were still visible and the smell of growing things hung in the air. There was a calm and mysterious quality to this morning, so we savored the here and now and were in no hurry, though we were due at a Christmas party hosted by our good friends in Reykjavík. I had yet to cut your hair, which I had mostly done since we lived in Copenhagen. At first it had been a way of saving money, but now I did it because no one else could cut it better. This was always quite a solemn undertaking, and you were so pleased with your haircuts, like a little boy, and usually said, "This looks really great." Yes, you got a great haircut that morning, such a good one that there was no need to cut or trim your hair for the funeral. That was already done, that was my masterpiece.

Just before we drove off that day, you mentioned that you didn't want to leave our summer house. I had the same feeling, but the party awaited and of course we would go. There was a strong sense of melancholy for both of us to leave the place this time. I can call this melancholy forth at any moment. On our way to town we bought a Christmas tree, something we always did well in advance. You were tired after the drive and took a nap at home just before we left for the party. I had to call you twice to wake you, which was unusual for a man who usually woke up at the slightest movement. I felt an unpleasant, restless sensation. Something was hanging in the air.

The party was a merry one, everyone happy and cheerful, and we enjoyed a delicious Christmas buffet in the Swedish style. We sat at the dinner table for a long time and you conversed at length with our host. I came to know later that you had spoken openly about your life and your satisfaction with it. You had said you felt you had accomplished what you had wished for in this life. I also found out later that you had told the woman on the farm closest to our summer house that when the time came, you wished to be laid to rest in the little country churchyard.

When the Christmas party was at its height and coffee and cognac were about to be served, you were in the middle of a sentence, praising a woman for her translations for Icelandic television. I sat diagonally across from you when you suddenly said the words "come home." And you said nothing else. At that very moment, your head moved back ever so slightly. Your face turned white, then grayish purple, and fell forward in a split second. I saw and knew immediately that you were dead. I immediately felt you were "so dead." It's hard to describe the feeling and experience of witnessing the death of another person. Watching him die. I knew it would be hopeless to resuscitate you and was opposed to it, but I had nothing to say about that, as nobody asked me. I was in a state of shock, completely speechless. The ambulance ride is all fog, and I have a vague recollection of a doctor at the hospital saying, "The man has passed away." Egill had said "come home," not "let's go home." But I was the one who went home alone.

At the funeral, I felt a deep and undefined need to stand up and speak. After the minister had read the eulogy, I stood up, walked to the coffin, and placed my hand on it. What I said was: "You gave me the closeness and warmth that I needed, you gave me sincere love and honesty. Because of this, my yearning for you will be easier to bear. Thank you, dear friend, rest in peace."

Was this perhaps life, then? - to have loved one summer in youth and not to have been aware of it until it was over, some sea-wet footprints on the floor and sand in the prints, the fragrance of a woman, soft loving lips in the dusk of a summer night, sea birds; and then nothing more; gone.

(World Light)

LIFE IS FRAGILE

Life gives, life takes, and life gives again.

In the beginning, we are all given an innate life force. This force gives birth to infinite possibilities of joy, love, enjoyment, experience, and discovery. We all search for happiness, yet none of us really knows what it consists of. Life often gives us joy without our mentioning it specially.

The default happiness that we had is no more. From now on, happiness will never be the default. A short time span separates what was and what has now suddenly taken its place. Isn't it remarkable that now when our spouse has passed away, we suddenly think of all those years we had together as happy years, without having paid them any attention at the time; and that now, in our suffering, life gives us a new understanding of how precious this shared life was?

Viktor E. Frankl, the famous Austrian psychiatrist, believes that each person must find their own individual purpose in life. He asserts that human beings can find a purpose in three ways: by loving; by working on some task; and through suffering. He suggests that if we do not see a purpose to our life now, we must search within ourselves for the will to find one.

There is so much more in us than we think. We own ourselves and we are our own companions. We possess far more strength than we realize. Therein lies our wealth of possibilities.

The world is constantly changing. Thus change is always on the horizon. We know it will come, but neither how nor when. We want to hold on to what we have, to what we own, to what we think we own. We don't want to lose anything. In truth we own nothing. We are only here on this earth for a short while and able to enjoy while we are here.

In her book *Life Lessons*, psychiatrist Elisabeth Kübler-Ross writes:

> *Change is saying good-bye to an old, familiar situation and facing a new, unfamiliar situation. Sometimes it's not the old or the new that unnerves us, it's the time in between. Ronnie Kaye, author of Spinning Straw into Gold and a two-time breast cancer survivor, says, "In life when one door closes, another door always opens ... but the hallways are a bitch. » That is how change works, it usually begins with a door closing, an ending, a completion, a loss, a death. Then we enter an uncomfortable period, mourning this completion and living in the uncertainty of what is next. This period of uncertainty is hard. But just when we feel we can't take it anymore, something new emerges: a reintegration, a reinvestment, a new beginning. A door opens. If you fight change, you will be fighting your whole life. That's why we need to find a way to embrace change, or at least to accept it.*

The relationship we had will never be taken from us. It lives forever within us. It is good to be grateful for having loved. It is good to be able to give thanks for being alive and getting to keep going.

Though the loss was great, grief painful, and the suffering deep, love made it all worthwhile.

PREFACE

The seed to the book Losing a Spouse is the story of Anna Ingolfs, who was thirty-five years old when she lost her husband, Árni Margeirsson, to cancer after a seven-month illness. He was thirty-nine . They have three daughters, who were four, six and twelve years old at the time. What makes Anna's story unique is that it is based on journals she kept during her husband's illness, and then after Árni passed away. Through the years, she wondered whether these journals should be made available to the public. The thought of publishing them grew more and more pressing. After becoming involved with a group of people who had lost their spouses, Anna realized how important it is for people in that situation to share their experience with others and acquire knowledge and understanding of the seriousness of losing a spouse. This motivated Anna to consider seriously the possibility of sharing her journals publicly.

Anna contacted Guðfinna Eydal, a respected psychologist in Iceland whom she knew by her professional reputation. She asked Guðfinna to read her journals. She knew that Guðfinna had several decades' experience as a clinical psychologist in private practice. Guðfinna had lost her husband, Egill Egilsson, about two years earlier. He had died suddenly of a heart attack at the age of sixty-seven.

Guðfinna was moved by Anna's story. After several discussions they decided to write a book together, containing also Guðfinna's short memoir of her marital life. The idea gradually evolved in the direction of a more substantial work on the loss of a spouse that would contain both accounts of real life experiences and discussion of psychological aspects of the matter. The book would thus appeal to a broader readership and could also serve as educational material.

The loss of a spouse is considered one of the most traumatic experiences that a person can go through. No two instances of grief are the same, and no two people suffer in the same way after losing their partner, though many threads of shared human experience may connect them. Such loss can have a serious impact on people's mental and physical health, and it is important for people to process their grief so that they can carry on with their lives. It is our hope that this book will be useful to people grieving a spouse, and that it will further be of use of all those who take an interest in the issue.

We have worked on this book in close cooperation for almost three years. In the course of this work, we have unavoidably shared sensitive experiences with each other. A great deal of material from our personal experiences is interwoven with the text. There was much laughing and crying as we wrote the book. For us, this work has been unique and rewarding and unlike any other project either of us has taken on.

Our division of labor in writing this book was that Anna contributed her story and wrote meditations. Guðfinna wrote her story, in addition to contributing text based on scientific research and scholarly knowledge. Both of us wrote the assignments, and together we made final adjustments to the manuscript. All case studies are fictional and no representation of actual people is intended.

We are very grateful for the opportunity to connect over this sensitive project. We were brought together by the experience that neither of us wanted to have, the experience of losing our husbands. We are grateful to have had the strength and courage to take this project on. We are convinced that this book is important and speaks to people of all ages around the world.

Hellholt, summer 2013

Anna Ingolfs, Gudfinna Eydal

I. THE LOVE AND THE LOSS

INTIMATE RELATIONSHIPS

Human beings form their deepest and strongest bonds with their parents, or other parental figures, in the earliest stages of life. Throughout our lives we have a need for intimate relationships. In adulthood, we form a deep bond with our spouses. The spousal relationship often takes over from the parental bond and can satisfy the human need for sincere love and happiness.

Healthy interactions with other people and deep bonding in early life contribute to mental health and stability. We learn to love ourselves and others, to give and to receive, as well as to place ourselves in others' shoes and empathize with them. A good relationship with a spouse, who is also our best friend and soul mate, gives us the opportunity to strengthen and deepen these important abilities. A good spouse is beyond compare, and her love is unconditional. She loves you as you are.

Ideally, your spouse is the person who knows you best of all, better than parents and best friends. She knows your strengths and weaknesses. You share nearly everything with your spouse and open yourself to her with sincerity and frankness. There is no performance going on, and you stand before her without any costumes or disguises. She gets to know those sides of your personality that you prefer to hide from others, even your children. Your spouse sees the naked reality of you. We often inhabit certain roles around other people and don't want them to know everything about us, neither our parents, friends, nor offspring. Over the course of a day we assume many different guises, depending on whom we interact with. We let go of these roles when we come home and step into the safety of our own space. Your home is the sanctuary where you don't have to play a part and your spouse knows you as you are.

Most of us desire to have a spouse and try to form intimate relationships. There are many reasons for this. International research has shown that those who live with a spouse are happier, live longer, and enjoy better health than those who do not. A good marriage is the best companionship imaginable for many different reasons.

(Love through Thick and Thin)

First, it is only in cohabitation that we can enjoy everything that companionship has to offer. Your husband or wife is at once your family, your best friend, and a companion for the long term. It's no wonder that the one who survives the loss of a spouse is disoriented. He or she loses so much.

Second, unlike other family ties and bonds of friendship, there is the sexual relationship between partners. This gives the relationship greater intimacy.

Third, there is equality between spouses in a good marriage, unlike other relationships that entail a certain inequality (e.g., parent and child, older and younger sibling).

Fourth, spouses are most often together every day. The continuous time people spend together leaves its mark and bonds them more closely. Women are often more aware of this than men and push for more time with their partner.

"Because the particular characteristics of the spousal relationship can fulfill such different and deep needs, not much can compare to a good marriage. But by the same token, few things are as harmful as a bad marriage, where the partners are unhappy. The choice of a spouse is thus among the most important decisions we make in life."

(Love through Thick and Thin)

LIFE CHANGES COLOR

The duration and quality of a spousal relationship affects how a surviving partner experiences and handles the loss. If your spouse was the most important person in your life and yours was a relationship of equals, it is likely that your grieving process will be less conflicted. It will be more marked by a profound sense of loss and longing. If the relationship was characterized by tension and disharmony, the processing may be even more difficult and the grief marked by inner conflict.

In a good relationship, the spouse has often played a part in raising her partner, nurturing self-respect and the belief that life is good and worth living. The spouse has given joy, support, encouragement, and help during hard times, been the best friend. She gave life special purpose.

When the spouse is gone, many will reminisce about the relationship and ask themselves all sorts of questions, such as: Was it attraction and love at first sight? How did the relationship evolve? Are there more memories of good times than bad, or vice versa? Were we similar or dissimilar from the beginning? Did we grow more alike with age? Did we keep the relationship going even though it wasn't very good? Were we always together even though we didn't connect particularly well? Did we grow together or in different directions? Was the spark there, could we find it from time to time, or was it perhaps completely gone? Were we always sure we wanted to be together, or did we doubt the relationship sometimes?

Losing a spouse can be like losing a part of yourself, and one might even say that when your spouse dies, a little bit of you also dies. Life changes color all of a sudden. The impact of the loss can be very strong at first, particularly if the death was sudden, as with a brief illness, an accident, or suicide. A great void is created.

PAT AND BOB

Pat, a 47-year-old lawyer, lost her husband Bob after a short illness of only three weeks. Though there was no time to discuss intimate concerns before the end came, Pat felt helped by the fact that she and her husband had often discussed death, not just in the context of their own mortality, but in a general sense. Pat described her husband with respect and characterized their relationship as one of equals. They were both open and expressed themselves easily, were friends and laughed a great deal together. When two couples close to them divorced, they felt how strong their bond was and were certain they would never divorce. They were both well educated and enjoyed respect in their professions. After the shock of losing Bob, Pat went through a period in which she felt she wasn't fully in control of her feelings and behavior. She felt anxious and had unprovoked crying jags. What surprised her most was that she began to be afraid of the dark and didn't feel able to sleep alone in her house. Her son and friend spent the night at her place by turns for seven months after Bob's death.

At first sight, most everything seems unchanged. I go to work as before, do the same tasks, meet the same people, and spend my time in the same places as before. Eat, sleep, chat.

But inside me is this feeling that rarely lets go. It is vague, some sort of an amalgam of fear and waiting in uncertainty. As if some threat is constantly hanging over me.

It is reminiscent of a toothache, but a toothache of the soul. It reminds me constantly that even though everything looks much like before, it is all changed. I am, too. Though I move, look, and behave like the one I was, I am not.

I miss myself and you and what was.

(I shall not want.)

THE LOVE FOR YOUR SPOUSE

Love and affection are things we all long for, but not everyone receives. If you were blessed with them and later lost your love, the grief will be great and the longing for what was will be almost unbearable. Nothing can destroy love that has been deep and strong, not even death. The surviving partner will continue to love his spouse, and sometimes it is possible to evoke a feeling of love after the loss that resembles the love you felt for her when she was alive and the strong desires you had when you first met. It can give you a certain feeling of pleasure to find such old, genuine feelings, but this can also evoke a deep sorrow for not having this life any longer. Now only the memories remain. But it can also be a source of joy and comfort to be able to access such precious memories.

On the other hand, small everyday occurrences can easily be a source of unpleasant emotions, confirming in a tangible way that your partner is gone. Just seeing couples holding hands in the street, dancing together, or shopping can bring out the tears. Meeting someone who reminds you of your husband or wife in appearance, manners or dress can be an immediate trigger for a deep sense of longing. Such events may continue to occur for years to come and can be a source of tears though a long time has passed since your loss.

The loss can cause a turmoil of vastly different emotions within you, reminding you of what you have lost and your present solitude. In your suffering, it is important to remember that you feel so much pain because you loved so dearly and were loved in return. Your spouse was your life. You experienced unconditional love and recognition of yourself as the person you are. The memory of that is a source of strength. You will always possess it, and it is unique to you. This memory will always be a part of you. It strengthens you in the belief that love and kindness make life worth living.

Icelandic writer and scholar S. Nordal (1886-1974) said of love: *He who wishes to rid himself of all grief and longing will have to pay the dear price of loving nothing in the world.*

JAN AND GERTRUD

Jan and Gertrud were just over fifty when they bought a summer house in a pleasant part of the countryside. It was only an hour's drive from their home, and they spent nearly every weekend there in the summer. They grew flowers and planted saplings, which they named and observed over the years as they grew into trees. They were never happier than when they were in the country. Jan often read books out loud to Gertrud while she knitted sweaters for their grandchildren. Gertrud loved to bring Jan breakfast in bed on Sunday mornings. After Gertrud dies in a car accident, Jan no longer feels able to go to the summer house. Though a year has passed since Gertrud's death, he has not been able to go to the house. There is no one there to read to, and breakfast in bed is a thing of the past. He misses Gertrud and their life together with unbearable pain.

WHEN YOUR PARTNER IS GONE

On losing a spouse, the bereaved partner can by no means cope with the sudden and unexpected loss and can do little to protect himself when the reactions overwhelm him. Past experiences are of little or no use. At first, you feel you have hardly any foundation to build on and experience great inner turmoil. Your mind is in a state of upheaval and your body can be consumed by it, rendered almost numb. All you can do now is to try to survive, one day at a time. The situation could be likened to a storm that rages where there seems to be no way out. All you can do is to wait and let it die down. You don't want to be caught in this storm, but for now there is nothing you can do but be there. The intensity of the weather will decrease slowly and gradually, but the gusts will still hit periodically.

Right after the loss, the first days will be consumed with absorbing the fact that your husband or wife has died. She is gone and won't come back, no matter how much you long for it, cry, or scream that you don't want this. Crying and sadness take over and your emotions become very volatile. Everything looks hopeless. This feeling seems to have come to stay. Then the clouds begin to part for a moment here and there, but the mood swings are great. Gradually, you will feel better, and most people feel more stable after the first year, though they usually still have a long way to go. This can be hard to believe at first. Many feel they will never make it out of their misery.

SUFFERING TAKES ITS TOLL

The loss of a spouse is considered one of the most serious emotional traumas a person can suffer. This explains why responses to such a loss are often so strong. Immediately after the spouse's death, many bereaved partners' situations are characterized by great heaviness and depression, numbness, frequent crying, difficulty sleeping, a change in appetite, fatigue, and ill health. Many are often tired and easily exhausted. Normal, everyday tasks prove difficult; it can be hard to get things done even when necessary. Some are even faced with the thought that they don't want to live anymore. At this point you often don't know how on Earth you will go about living without your spouse. As time goes by and things begin to stabilize, you can try to be more conscious of your emotions and reactions. You will gradually regain your bearings and become more able to take responsibility and make personal decisions.

Grief causes stress to the body, which can sometimes threaten your mental and physical health. Mental state influences physical balance and vice versa. Grief weakens our defenses. It can cause health crises, both temporary and long-term. The responses of the autonomic nervous system are strong, and it is difficult for the body when responses to stress become dominant. The situation is especially serious just after the bereavement and in the following days and weeks. The probability of a heart attack can increase. It is therefore vital for the surviving spouse to try to acknowledge what has happened and look for ways to improve his own well-being. It is necessary to adapt to new circumstances and to release gradually those strong emotions attached to the deceased.

The loss can also have an extensive impact on the mental health of the deceased partner's children and parents, and can affect the emotional state of close friends and colleagues. Professional support can be invaluable for others in the inner circle, as well as for the bereaved him- or herself.

Grief seeks release, and if we try to deny it, it will take its toll. For instance, it can lead to anxiety and depression. Repressing grief can also increase the likelihood that we will be drawn to unfortunate ways of handling our feelings, like anti-anxiety medications, sleeping pills, alcohol, and other drugs.

In grief, suffering is inescapable – we must accept it, suffer it, go through it, and wrestle with it. We must give suffering time and neither run from it nor deny it. We must face our suffering and try to understand that it is the only way out of grief.

In the first year after your loss, you will have to shoulder the responsibility for everything on your own for the first time. You have to take over various practical responsibilities that used to fall to your partner, such as household maintenance or taking the car for inspections. You now have to organize all vacations on your own and take sole charge of once-shared tasks, such as grocery shopping. You may have moments where you think, "This time last year, she wasn't dead." Many feel that after the first year, a certain circle is closed, and find it a bit easier to do things the second time. Yet it's not uncommon for grieving spouses to describe the second year as even more difficult. After the struggle of the first year, the longing for the lost loved one emerges with greater force.

Many learn gradually to live with the loss and are able to shape a new pattern to their lives. Others struggle to accomplish that, and some never fully recover and live out the rest of their lives in great grief. A few even give up on life and die shortly after their partners. Therefore, it is vitally important to become familiar with various aspects of losing a spouse and to try to understand why it is such a serious trauma to those who suffer it.

TIME DOESN'T HEAL ALL WOUNDS

We don't like to dwell too much on the possibility of losing someone we love. The thought that someone might die and leave us behind is not only uncomfortable, but can be downright anxiety-inducing. For this reason, we often push such thoughts away. We don't want to acknowledge them, but deep down inside we all know that sooner or later we will lose someone close to us. Grief will come knocking at some point in life, and we will stand exposed. Most of us lose our parents, some lose a child, friends, or relatives, and many lose a spouse.

In marital relationships, the odds that one spouse will predecease the other are overwhelming. We don't know when or how that will happen. The loss may occur in a very different way and at a different time from what we can imagine. A person who wakes up healthy one morning may die before nightfall. We have no choice but to accept what life hands us in these matters.

The old adage is that time heals all wounds. It's not quite that simple, as everyone knows who has been through painful grief. Time does change grief, however, and with the passage of time it doesn't disturb us as much. Grief changes us. Through grief we can become aware of how precious love is and how important other people are to us. We are better able to see important values in life, to identify what really matters to us. We also have the opportunity to gain self-knowledge through grief, because it forces us to look ourselves in the eye in a new way. We can learn to know who we are independently of our spouse. This can be a difficult experience for many, particularly those who have spent a long life together and been very dependent on each other. Upon losing our partner, we sometimes discover that we are more sensitive and fragile in some areas than we thought. On the other hand, we may also discover that we are stronger and more capable than we expected – we can simply do more. Our responses and emotions can be surprising, not least when we have to go the distance through day after day of unhappiness and ask ourselves questions that may never be answered.

Time goes on, but it has a different meaning than before. There is no longer such a rush. Life runs its course. Living in the moment becomes more important, receiving each day as a gift, enjoying while we can.

BETTY AND MATT

Betty visited a psychologist just under two years after her husband Matt died. She felt her recovery from the loss was taking much too long and was worried at her perpetual sadness and lack of interest in anything. She found life rather pointless and felt more dissatisfied with work after Matt's death. The psychologist helped Betty recall a number of events that had occurred in her life, and they discussed her relationship with Matt. When the psychologist asked her point blank whether she'd had any dreams before she met Matt, Betty's eyes lit up. After a brief hesitation, Betty said that she had always wanted to create something from yarn and try to sell it. She revealed that she had received prizes for her handicrafts while in school, and at a school exhibition her creations attracted special attention. As Betty reminisced about this, a twinkle of joy was apparent in her eyes, and at the psychologist's encouragement she decided to explore the possibility further. Betty's interest in life gradually grew, and she began to see the possibility of making an old dream come true. She started to revive old ideas and amass new ones, and began to make beautiful and unique objects from yarn. Little by little, she presented her creations to others, and two years later she founded a small company for her products. She wrote the psychologist a letter expressing her thanks.

II. MAN AND GRIEF

EVERYONE GRIEVES DIFFERENTLY

The grieving process is always personal. No two individuals respond in the same way. People are in different places in life, their ages differ, and their losses happen in different ways. Some have small children, others adult ones, and yet others have no children at all. Some have a large network of family and friends, others have few close confidants. People's financial circumstances differ, and difficult financial circumstances at the time of bereavement increase the anxiety and stress felt by the surviving partner. The grieving process can be more difficult if the surviving partner has been dealing with physical or mental illness of her own before her spouse died. Responses to grief are thus dependent on many diverse and complex factors.

In order to gain a better understanding of your own situation at the time of your loss, it may be interesting for you to consider a few questions concerning yourself in the aftermath of the loss. The list below is not exhaustive, but can give some ideas.

- Am I sensitive, perhaps hypersensitive?
- Do I have a tendency toward anxiety?
- Do I get angry easily? Do I have difficulty setting boundaries?
- Can I talk to some people but not others?

- Do I find it easy or difficult to communicate, or do I burn up inside with emotions that I can't put into words?
- Do I handle solitude well or badly?
- Am I a more independent person, or am I dependent on others?
- Do I find ways out of trouble easily, or can I not see any ways out?
- Do I become helpless easily?
- What is my personality?
- Am I an open or a closed person?
- What pattern do my reactions follow?
- How old was I when I lost my partner?
- What was the cause of death?
- How long was our relationship?
- What was my relationship with my spouse like?
- Was it characterized by stability, or were there conflicts?
- Was I very dependent on my husband/wife?
- Do I have children/Am I childless?
- How is my mental and physical health?
- Have I suffered other losses or traumatic experiences?
- What is my support network like?
- How is my relationship with my own family and my husband's/wife's family?
- Do I have good friends?
- How are my finances?
- Do I find solitude easy or difficult?

A MEASURE OF STRESS

The following is a list based on research conducted in Seattle, Washington, USA. Known as the Holmes and Rahe Stress Scale, the list assigns a value in so-called "life change units" to stressful events in a person's life. This number indicates how great a negative impact the event can have on the health of the person in question. Those who accumulate 150 to 300 units in a year are more likely to have a health crisis within three months than those who have fewer units.

Life Event	Life Change Units
Death of a spouse	100
Divorce	73
Marital separation	65
Imprisonment	63
Death of a close family member	63
Personal injury or illness	53
Marriage	50
Dismissal from work	47
Marital reconciliation	45
Retirement	45
Change in health of family member	44
Pregnancy	40
Sexual difficulties	39
Gain a new family member	39
Business readjustment	39
Change in financial state	38

Life Event	Life Change Units
Death of a close friend	37
Change to different line of work	36
Change in frequency of arguments	35
Major mortgage	32
Foreclosure of mortgage or loan	30
Change in responsibilities at work	29
Child leaving home	29
Trouble with in-laws	29
Outstanding personal achievement	28
Spouse starts or stops work	26
Begin or end school	26
Change in living conditions	25
Revision of personal habits	24
Trouble with boss	23
Change in working hours or conditions	20
Change in residence	20
Change in schools	20
Change in recreation	19
Change in church activities	19
Change in social activities	18
Minor mortgage or loan	17
Change in sleeping habits	16
Change in number of family reunions	15
Change in eating habits	15
Vacation	13
Christmas	12
Minor violation of law	11

(Holmes and Rahe, 1967)

JOHN AND ROSIE

John was 53 years old when he lost his job, just half a year before his wife Rosie suddenly passed away of a stroke. His unemployment hit him hard and affected his self-confidence severely. He suddenly felt useless and feared he would never be able to re-enter the job market. The future seemed bleak. John was seriously concerned about their finances, but as Rosie had a well-paying job he thought they would pull through. With Rosie's death John's life is turned completely upside down. Two weeks after her passing, he has to be checked into a hospital with cardiac arrhythmia and high blood pressure.

A NATURAL RESPONSE TO LOSS

Grief has not been given the place it is due in Western culture. We seek to avoid it and find it difficult to talk openly about feelings related to grief. We try to push them away as swiftly as possible, wishing grief to be over as soon as may be. Many societies seem not to accept well enough that the processing of grieving takes time. Many mourners therefore experience the silent demand of society that they "should" be further along in their grieving process than they really are. But grief doesn't follow some timeline. It runs its course in its own time, and trying to force out different emotions can disturb the process. It is illogical to expect that grief should be over at certain point, or that the grieving person "should be recovered by now," because the processing of grief does not obey such simple laws.

The fast pace of modern life leaves little space for grief. We learn a great deal about how to obtain things and what is considered important in life. We are supposed to have a home and a family, we are supposed to get an education and a suitable job, make friends and have hobbies. The emphasis is on construction, consumption, and future plans. We are taught much less, however, about what to do when we lose much of what is dearest to us, our nearest relatives, our health, or material comforts. When that happens, we find ourselves exposed, alone, without anything to hold on to, and don't know how or where to turn.

The most important thing to realize is that grief is a natural response to having lost. This applies to the loss of a loved one, divorce, natural disasters, loss of employment, and loss of financial security.

COMMON RESPONSES TO LOSS

Just as all relationship are unique, so are responses to the loss of a spouse. Still, people's psychological and physical reactions to losing their partners are most often similar and reflect a common human experience. Everyone who goes through an emotional crisis and deep grief must deal with some, if not all, of these reactions. Their duration can vary, but some of them are strongest at first. It matters for many to get support after their bereavement. Some are in great need of support for a short time, but others may need long-term assistance. The surviving spouse often has to seek out all this help herself and doesn't always know where it is best to look.

Some divorces elicit similar responses to the loss a spouse. This is particularly true when one partner leaves the relationship with almost no warning, after beginning an affair. The one who is left behind is in absolute shock, doesn't want to accept what has happened or to face the consequences. In both cases the wife/husband is no longer there. In one situation, s/he is alive, yet gone nonetheless. In the other, s/he is no longer alive.

SHOCK AND NUMBNESS

Many find themselves almost numb just after the death of their spouse, especially if the death was sudden. The first response is to try to protect yourself from what has happened. It is not possible to absorb the message and all the pain at once. Some surviving partners become numb and paralyzed. Others resist forcefully. The pain is overwhelming. Numbness is the body's way to protect us from the shock that has befallen us. The numbness then recedes and the mourner can gradually begin to recognize the reality of the loss. This numbness is usually strongest in the first hours and days after the loss, and its strength varies from person to person.

CONCENTRATION DISTURBANCES

The mourner may have difficulty concentrating on other projects and be preoccupied with the loss. Many suffer memory loss and cannot retain everyday information. These may be simple occurrences like going to fetch something from the fridge and not being able to remember what it was, forgetting what your errand to the storage closet was, or being out behind the wheel and having no recollection of where you are driving to.

UNREAL PERCEPTIONS AND HYPERSENSITIVITY

The mourner may often feel that the deceased spouse is nearby. She may feel that her spouse is coming in through the door or is in the living room. The surviving spouse may also feel her partner's touch or smell. It is not unusual for a person who misses someone painfully and longs for her deeply to experience a sort of virtual reality at first. As time goes by, these unreal perceptions will become less incursive, and they usually vanish with time.

Many mourners feel themselves becoming hypersensitive to the least stimulus. All sorts of sounds may become overwhelming, slipping through flesh and bone in ways the mourner had never experienced before. It is as if the senses are constantly on alert. The mourner may jump at the least provocation and can tolerate various external stimuli much less than before.

KENDRA AND CHARLES

When Kendra went back to work, four months after losing her spouse, she still felt from time to time like her husband, Charles, was still alive. She often jumped when the phone rang at the end of the workday and felt that it must be Charles calling. For a moment it struck her that she might have dreamed the whole thing and nothing had really happened. That everything was just fine, it was all in her head, Charles was still alive and would come home from work just after her, like he had always done.

MOOD SWINGS AND ANGER

Many mourners find that their moods fluctuate considerably. Some experience irritation, get frustrated at the least provocation and have little tolerance for adversity.

Unrest and inner turmoil can be intense. Sometimes the tears take over, and it seems they will never abate. Anger is a part of many people's responses to losing a spouse, but not everyone's. Some direct their anger at doctors, nurses, and even God. Some mourners' moods oscillate between anger and depression.

Melancholy or boundless sorrow can follow the loss of a spouse. Emotions can be strong and conflicting. Sometimes people feel a certain relief that their partner's struggles are at an end and his suffering at an end. At the same time, the surviving partner may feel despair at the thought of being alone and no longer having a beloved spouse by her side.

THE NEED FOR SUPPORT

The mourner's need for companionship in the wake of the loss can vary greatly and is often dependent on her emotional state and mood swings. At first she may want to have her nearest family and friends with her most of the time, but be left alone otherwise. It is important for her support network to recognize such reactions, to be understanding of them, and to consider them normal. This shows the grieving spouse tolerance and empathy. Family and friends must realize that despite their desire to be supportive, they can only ever be on the sidelines.

CHANGES IN EATING HABITS

The emotional upheaval can affect eating habits. Some have difficulty eating and lose almost all appetite. Others respond in the opposite way and turn to food for comfort. Yet others may swing between these two extremes.

IRREGULAR SLEEP

Grief after losing a spouse almost always affects sleep. Many who have always slept well will now experience changes in their sleep patterns. They struggle to fall asleep and their sleep is irregular and restless. Many wake up in the middle of the night and don't fall asleep again until early morning, only to get up exhausted. Disturbed sleep can increase fatigue, irritation, and sadness. Some struggle with nightmares. Many long to dream of their late spouse and are disappointed if they don't. The need to sleep long hours may increase. The same individual may sleep too much and too little by turns. Sleep has a profound impact on mental health. It is difficult to have to deal with irregular sleep on top of everything else in the wake of a loss. Sometimes people use sleeping pills and anti-anxiety medications while dealing with grief. This may prove necessary at first to allow the mourner to meet their basic needs for sleep and relaxation. But if such medications are taken for an extended period of time, they may become addictive and interfere with the grieving process.

PHYSICAL SYMPTOMS AND LOW ENERGY

The impact of losing a spouse may manifest itself in strong physical symptoms just after the loss. Examples include shortness of breath, an irregular heartbeat, a feeling of suffocation, bodily aches, vomiting, and diarrhea. Difficult thoughts and emotions that stir within the mourner may sap her strength. Grieving partners often speak of great fatigue, describing themselves as exhausted and weak. Such sensations may also be present even when sleep is fairly regular. The energy and zest for life that the mourner had before is no longer there. This may feel like an additional loss on top of the bereavement.

ORANGE HANDS

I see your beautiful thick hands
I often saw them by the orange press
when one hand pressed on the other
the beautiful hands that did so much and could do so much
I see them still

(*Eydal G.*)

MISSING YOUR SPOUSE

You may miss your partner so powerfully that the sensation is almost like physical pain. At first almost everything reminds you of your spouse and you are constantly aware of your aloneness. Many mourners speak aloud to their deceased partner in order to lighten the burden. You may ask his advice or tell him how much you miss him.

It can be difficult for you as the surviving spouse if you had no chance to say goodbye to your husband or wife. Getting an opportunity to say your goodbyes is extremely significant. It helps you on the road to accepting the fact that your spouse is gone. When the loss strikes out of the blue, there is no chance to say goodbye. The surviving partner is then often left with the feeling that something is unfinished. That feeling can last a long time and may never go completely away. It seems we can find more inner peace by saying something beautiful at the end and perhaps hearing our spouse express something he wanted to say.

The longing for your spouse is tied up with many events and occasions. Family members' birthdays can be difficult, not least your husband's/wife's birthday. The first wedding anniversary after the bereavement can be characterized by tears from dawn till dusk. Major events like the birth of a child in the family, school graduations, and weddings always remind you that someone is missing. Certain times of year are often more difficult. The first major holiday alone, such as Passover, Christmas, Ramadan or Diwali, may cause you to miss your partner acutely, and summer vacations that used to be something to look forward to are now a source of anxiety. You may also miss painfully the feeling of being part of the unit you formed with your spouse. Everything we had to do together is gone, everything we loved to do together is gone too. Now it's just I, not we.

YOUR PERSONAL RELATIONSHIP WITH YOUR PARTNER

The surviving partner will become gradually more aware of what her loss really means to her. She begins to realize that she can no longer consult her spouse, nor can she share her feelings and sensitive personal matters with anyone the way she could before. She cannot talk about herself, her feelings, opinions, and interactions with other people in the same way as before. You simply don't trust anyone like you trusted your partner. With the death of your spouse, the personal relationship between the two of you has come to an end. Now you see more clearly how precious and personal this bond was and what you have really lost.

With the loss of a spouse, you lose the bond and the communication that once was. The embraces, kisses, warmth, compliments on clothing or appearance, sexual intimacy, and most of all the unconditional love is gone and no one will give it again in the same way.

Your loyal supporter, who always stood by you, encouraged you, took the blows and protected you if need be, is no longer there.

With the loss of your partner, your closest confidant is gone, the one you could always trust and talk to about anything, no matter how absurd. Your spouse's support was always there. He listened attentively, but could also allow himself to say that enough was enough and could criticize you. You each embraced the other, warts and all, and knew each other's strengths and weaknesses.

Spouses often speak a similar language. Over the years you spent together, you became more and more alike. You often didn't have to use many words to express things. Your partner understood immediately what you meant and often knew exactly how you were feeling. Your conversation often revolved mostly around your mutual interests. Some things were never brought up, because each party knew that the other had no interest in discussing them. The sense of humor was often similar and gave the relationship increased depth and strength. The surviving partner must bid all these things farewell.

When your husband/wife is gone, you can no longer plan for the future together, or share everything that goes on in life. The time you had together as a couple is gone, and now you can no longer reminisce together about sad and happy times from the past.

NOW YOU ARE GONE

In a cold winter
the staring house
with empty eyes
as I come home
in the darkness
now you're not here
I open the door
only silence and darkness
I close the door behind me
and I burst into tears

(Eydal G)

SENSITIVE EMOTIONS

Certain emotions can be particularly sensitive for a surviving spouse. They often cause great inner conflict. The spouse may feel negative emotions and various kinds of guilt toward the deceased. These emotions can be so sensitive and private that she may not feel able to discuss them directly with others.

ANGER AT THE SPOUSE

Anger can have many causes. The spouse left without permission, wasn't allowed to go and wasn't supposed to. The survivor is left alone and abandoned. The surviving partner may be angry at the other for not having taken good enough care of himself, perhaps for neglecting to go to the doctor despite constant reminders and being careless with his health. The bereaved partner may also be angry that the deceased spouse robbed her of the future she had expected them to have together.

Anger can also be directed inward. The surviving one may be angry at herself for various reasons. She may feel she should have been more supportive of her spouse and listened more attentively. She may also be angry at herself for having been inconsiderate of her partner, for having placed undue burdens on him by not contributing enough to tasks that could have been shared.

SUSAN AND HARRY

Susan loses her husband after a short illness. She and Harry began seeing each other around the age of forty and have lived together for fifteen years. They have no children together, but each has a child from a previous marriage. Their relationship has been good on the whole and they haven't suffered any particular blows, except that Susan has lost both her parents. Their relationships with the children have always been good, and there is great grief in the family when Harold suddenly passes away. He was a kind and good man. Susan did often worry that they lived beyond their means, but Harold usually avoided talking about money matters. He often said, "It'll be fine" if she voiced her concerns. In truth Susan hasn't taken much interest in their finances and doesn't know exactly how they are doing on that front. She does know that they still owe a fair amount on the house. Now it comes to light that Harold owed substantial sums that

Susan was unaware of. She anticipates difficult times and is afraid she may lose the house. She starts to feel fear of the future. Soon her fear becomes mixed with increasing feelings of anger towards Harry. She feels that his carelessness is now the reason for her poor circumstances. She is also angry at herself for not having been more responsible about financial matters.

GUILT TOWARDS THE SPOUSE

Anger and guilt can go hand in hand. The surviving spouse may be angry at herself for not having loved her partner enough. She may feel guilty that she didn't express her love more clearly. You can feel guilty over all manner of things, great and small: for example, having been too critical of your partner, negative in conversations, argumentative and fault-finding. People can feel guilty over financial matters, such as for having spent too much money or not having been a good enough provider.

When a spouse dies from illness, it is not uncommon for the surviving partner to accuse herself of not having seen soon enough where things were headed and even for not having been caring enough during the illness. The grieving spouse may feel guilty for having advised her partner something that proved incorrect, for having downplayed things that later proved important, or for not having listened carefully enough to something the sick partner reiterated over and over again. It can weigh heavily on the surviving one to have made a promise she couldn't keep before her partner died.

Regardless of what form the guilt takes, it usually revolves around the surviving partner's feeling that she could have made her spouse happier and been more supportive if certain things had been done or not done. In that case, her spouse might not have died. By accusing herself like this in the context of losing a spouse, the grieving partner is often trying to convince herself that she could have exerted some control over her partner's death.

ROBERT AND DORA

Robert and Dora have lived together for thirty-two years. Dora works independently as a business consultant. She is an anxious woman and has often consulted a doctor because of this. Robert feels she medicates too often and with insufficient reason. He has been concerned about this for quite some time, as well as about her drinking. Dora responds badly to Robert's comments. Her use of drugs and alcohol gradually increases, and Robert insists that she seek help and treatment. Their grown children support their father completely and encourage their mother to get help. Dora shows little interest in taking their advice and doesn't think her problem is as serious as they do. Her drinking increases and she is often obviously drunk, both at home and at social gatherings, and even when she is alone. Dora has been a fairly steady worker, but she takes an increasing number of sick days, especially around weekends. Husband and wife's communication deteriorates. One day when Robert comes home from work fairly late, he finds Dora in their bedroom, barely responsive. He calls an ambulance, but Dora is declared dead on arrival at the hospital. After the funeral, Robert becomes overwhelmed by guilt and thinks that if he hadn't worked overtime on this particular day, Dora might still be alive. He regrets that he often blamed her for her drinking and now he feels sad for not having been able to understand how bad Dora really felt.

WHEN DEATH IS A RELIEF

In some cases, the surviving partner may feel a certain relief on the death of the spouse. This may happen for various reasons, particularly if the spouse was very ill or suffered for a long time. The survivor is relieved that the battle with the disease is over. You no longer have to watch your partner wither away, losing his dignity and most of his characteristics.

When your spouse has suffered severe damage from an accident or a stroke and it is evident that recovery is impossible, you may hope that your partner is allowed to die. Your spouse's passing can thus come as a great relief. If your spouse has been violent or if negative feelings towards him are strong, his death may come as a certain liberation to you. The same may be the case if your partner was addicted to drugs or alcohol.

When death comes as a relief, guilt and shame at feeling partly happy over what has happened are often not far behind. This can make the grief even more difficult to process.

JAMES AND BETH

Beth and James have been together for over twenty years when Beth dies suddenly of a heart attack. They have two teenagers in the household. Their relationship had been stormy, and James connected this principally with Beth's explosive temper. She could erupt over the smallest things and often scolded him excessively. Sometimes she lost control of herself completely. Living with her had often been extremely trying. But these were behaviors that James knew Beth only engaged in at home. After recovering from the worst of the shock of Beth's death, James begins to feel a certain relief. Home has become peaceful. James is half-ashamed of his feelings and tells himself that he has no right to feel relieved when his wife has just passed away. When James hears friends and family mention what a close and supportive couple they were, his heart aches and he finds himself thinking hard about his own feelings.

"That is the secret of happiness and virtue – liking what you've got to do."

(Brave New World)

THE NEARNESS OF DEATH

Since the dawn of time, mankind has pondered its fate. The big questions of life and death have followed us since the beginning. We wonder where we came from, why we are here on Earth, where we're going and what will happen to us when we leave this Earthly life. These eternal questions will probably follow us for as long as life continues.

One of our deepest fears is probably the fear of death. It is natural to fear what we do not understand. This is not least true of a phenomenon as complex as death. This fear is common to all humanity. Many people don't share their views on death with others, as death isn't a frequent topic of conversation for most of us. We usually try to discuss it as little as possible until it appears in some way. Perhaps for this reason we agree so well to try to kill it with silence until it arrives.

Some have a very decisive attitude toward death. Others' views vacillate more. Some believe death to be an absolute end to life. Everything ends. When the body dies, the soul dies with it. Some believe in God and believe they will achieve eternal life after death. Some also believe that the soul will remain alive after bodily death. Yet others believe that a person will be reborn repeatedly in new bodies.

On losing a spouse, death comes very close to us. This nearness makes the surviving partner involuntarily more aware of her own mortality and may lead her to fear her own death. Even if nothing suggests that death is near at hand, these thoughts can lead surviving partners to make provisions for their own death, for example by making a will and discussing their own funeral arrangements.

Some may wish that they themselves die soon after their bereavement so they can be reunited quickly with their spouse. Such wishes are usually strongest right after the loss.

Many grieving partners feel they age rapidly after their loss. People become more conscious of their age somehow. A person of about sixty whose spouse has passed away may feel she herself does not have so many days left to live. She may now feel quite old, even though she previously gave hardly a thought to her age.

Though we move closer to death with every passing moment, the feeling of denial toward it is generally strong. It is hard to reconcile with a fast and stressful life, wanting to have and enjoy as much as possible – which then suddenly ends one day. The finality is absolute. Is it strange, then, that death should strike us so harshly when it appears? We find ourselves naked and defenseless. We can no longer avoid the fact that death is a part of life. The loss of a loved one forces each one of us to recognize death, whether we wish to or not. Death changes life. Death changes you.

LEARNING TO HANDLE GRIEF

All theories on trauma, grief, and emotional crisis agree that grief must be processed in order for a person to recover from a trauma. Grief processing is based on a few challenges or tasks.

(The Psychology of Private Life.)

- **The first** task is to recognize the loss and face the trauma that has occurred. It takes time to accept reality, because it requires you not only to understand and accept the knowledge intellectually, but also to accept it emotionally.
- **The second** task is to recognize your suffering and work through it. Emotional and physical pain cannot be avoided, and so it is necessary to grapple with it directly.
- **The third** task is to adapt to your new circumstances without the spouse. Here you will be confronted not only with how much you miss your partner, but also with your nostalgia for what you had together. This demands a reevaluation of your own situation based on changed premises.
- **The fourth** task is to find a place for your spouse and go on with your life, to feel inside yourself that your late spouse has a special place in your heart and that the precious memory of him will live forever. The memory of you together will always be a part of life. Each bereaved

partner must gradually find the breathing room to examine what is the best way forward and find her own path. That can take time.

Clues to suggest that the surviving spouse is making good progress in the grieving process are on the one hand that in daily life, she is no longer consumed with a need to dwell on strong and fraught memories of her spouse, and on the other, that she can find the strength and enthusiasm to engage with life again.

UNRESOLVED ISSUES

There is often not an opportunity to resolve emotional issues before the spouse's death. This is often true when the death is sudden, for instance in cases of suicide or short illness. Sometimes a spouse on his deathbed doesn't want to discuss things, neither emotional issues nor his impending death. It may never have been easy to discuss sensitive emotional matters in the relationship, and perhaps death has never come up. Now as the end draws near, it may be even more difficult to take such matters up, and many feel it is too late. Both partners may now feel the need to speak and express themselves, especially the one who sees her spouse lie dying. She feels insecure about expressing herself now, both for fear of not saying what she has to say in the right way, and because she fears the consequences it may have for her partner. Neither partner wishes to burden the other in the final hour. Many matters may thus be left unresolved. They can therefore continue to burden the surviving partner.

Grief that is not processed can continue to cause problems and may affect your mental health. Unresolved grief may relate to difficult and painful past experiences. It can be born of not having expressed yourself enough to your spouse in a positive way, such as by telling him how important he was to you, how much you loved him, and how valued he was. Unprocessed grief may also be connected with feelings like regret over not having been somehow kinder and better to the lost loved one or having hurt him in some way, even over not having apologized for some past hurt. The spouse's death can engender an extremely strong urge to apologize and be forgiven or to release anger.

PROCESSING OF GRIEF BRINGS ACCEPTANCE AND PEACE

By facing grief, the mourner gradually moves in a positive direction. Emotional health improves and sadness gives way to more joy. The desire to live grows. Concentration improves and energy reserves grow.

IN THE PROCESSING OF GRIEF, YOU WILL FIND:

- **More acceptance** – You face facts, recognize the loss, and gradually come to accept your position.
- **Emotional balance** – The processing helps you work through the suffering, which in turn increases emotional balance.
- **A new emotional bond** – By facing the challenges of grief, you will

forge a new emotional bond with your late spouse, one that is based on love and a combination of grief, joy, and especially gratitude for having had just this exact spouse. This emotional transformation enables you to let go and move on with your life.

- **Renewed energy and interest in life** – When you can approach memories of your late spouse without their being too difficult or painful, your energy and interest in life will grow.

BERNHARD AND FIONA

Bernhard noticed when he no longer felt the sting of pain and sensitivity when his bridge partners mentioned his wife, Fiona, who had succumbed to cancer a year earlier. He felt that for all he still missed Fiona acutely, he liked meeting his friends and looked forward to their evenings more and more. He wasn't always in the best state, and it happened that he felt so awful that he wanted to stand up and leave in the middle of a game. Yet he never allowed himself to do that, deciding to stay and finish the evening. The company was that important to him. Bernhard gradually realized that he wanted to participate in life - that life had to go on, no matter what.

THE ART OF HELPING OTHERS TO UNDERSTAND

If One Is Truly to Succeed in Leading a Person to a Specific Place, One Must First and Foremost Take Care to Find Him Where He Is and Begin There.

This is the secret in the entire art of helping.

Anyone who cannot do this is himself under a delusion if he thinks he is able to help someone else. In order truly to help someone else, I must understand more than he – but certainly first and foremost understand what he understands.

If I do not do that, then my greater understanding does not help him at all. If I nevertheless want to assert my greater understanding, then it is because I am vain or proud, then basically instead of benefiting him I really want to be admired by him.

But all true help begins with a humbling.

The helper must first humble himself under the person he wants to help and thereby understand that to help is not to dominate but to serve, that to help is not to be the most dominating but the most patient, that to help is a willingness for the time being to put up with being in the wrong and not understanding what the other understands.

Søren Kierkegaard (1813 – 1855)

THE HYPERSENSITIVE SURVIVING SPOUSE

The loss of a spouse can render the surviving partner hypersensitive and weaken his emotional defenses significantly. He may be hurt by a variety of things that he would not react to in the same way under normal circumstances. Comments that may seem normal to people who are emotionally balanced may push a grieving spouse's buttons, shock him and anger him. He is that easily hurt. An innocent question like "Aren't you beginning to feel better?" may, in the aftermath of the loss, be a source of anguish and considerable introspection. Questions a few months after the partner's death, such as "Don't you think it's time for you to go back to work?" or "Aren't you getting over this?" may be just as hurtful to the mourner. He cannot answer such questions but often senses that they contain a veiled implication that the grief should come to an end. A grieving spouse may experience this as criticism of the life he lives now, shortly after the loss. It can often be better to communicate directly with the mourner and say, "It's good to see you, I think about you a lot and I hope you're doing well." When people have gained some distance from the most difficult grief, it is more empathetic to say, "You're looking really good," instead of saying, "You look much better, it's like night and day from before."

LIZ AND GILBERT

Liz does not feel ready to return to work even though three months have passed since Gilbert's death. She thinks constantly about the fateful day when they had a big fight about their finances, which was still unresolved when Gilbert had a sudden heart attack.

He was kept on life support for seven days until it became apparent that he would not wake up again. Liz has not been able to rest or sleep since his heart attack. She has been to see a doctor several times and has taken prescription sleeping pills to help herself rest. An acquaintance of Liz's works in the doctor's office and was very supportive when Liz first began coming for doctor's appointments. The friend says she would love to catch up with her and have her over for dinner. She reiterates this two or three times, yet the dinner invitation never materializes.

THE NEED TO EXPRESS THOUGHTS AND FEELINGS

A grieving spouse usually feels the need to talk about both what has happened and how he feels. He often wants to go on and on and recall the same things again and again. He may feel the need to recall the sequence of events in great detail. First and foremost, the spouse wants someone he trusts to listen to him. He doesn't necessarily need others' opinions or answers to the questions he asks, nor is he looking for any particular response to what he has to say. The primary issue is for himself to have an opportunity to communicate.

In the early days, some feel the need to elevate their lost loved one, repeatedly describing their spouse as practically perfect. The partner was so brilliant, knew so much and could do everything. The surviving spouse exaggerates the virtues of his late partner. With the passage of time, this estimation of the late spouse becomes more realistic, and consequently it becomes more possible to mention the spouse's faults and even joke about them.

It can be a source of great support to a surviving spouse who wishes to ponder death and dying if his nearest and dearest feel comfortable talking about this sensitive matter. In the shadow of death, the mourner's need to talk about it can become very strong. Some grieving partners wish to know what others think of death and are perhaps looking for a clearer picture within themselves of what death really means. Many feel the need to discuss religious matters with others and to compare their own opinions and ideas with those of others.

SENSITIVE RELATIONSHIPS AFTER LOSS

Most people who lose a spouse receive support and compassion from others. It is invaluable to have good friends and family who are there for you when the need is great. Upon the loss of a spouse, everyone needs sympathy and compassion. Despite the best intentions of friends and family, mourners are not all equally able to hear words of encouragement, such as that it will all get better after a certain amount of time, that it feels the worst in the beginning, that perhaps this was all for the best, since the spouse had suffered so much and is now "in a better place." Nor is it appropriate to tell a grieving spouse that it is a blessing to die a sudden death or to mention that most people wish to die in such a way.

Just after death, many people who are close to the bereaved spouse find it difficult to interact with him. They feel insecure about how they should behave and what is appropriate for them to say. "Should I visit him often or seldom? Should I call every day or a few times a week? Should I leave him mostly alone and let him be in touch if he wants to?" There are no simple answers to these questions, because everyone's emotional state and need for connection is so different during this phase. Many friends and family members also fear that they will have a difficult time handling the grieving spouse's possible responses, such as crying, losing control, or even becoming inconsolable. Others fear they will cry themselves or be unable to handle unexpected circumstances.

Sometimes friends and family choose to withdraw for some time after the funeral. There may be many reasons for that. They may think the surviving spouse needs time to himself in order to recover from the shock. Many relatives and friends may feel they don't have the strength to meet the surviving partner while the grief is at its heaviest.

Because of their own limited knowledge of grief responses, it may come as a surprise to family and friends to see how the mourning spouse reacts when they approach him in the first weeks after the shock. The mourner's responses may fluctuate wildly in ways that are highly uncharacteristic for him. At this time, he can't disguise how he feels. He may be irritated, cry, be sullen, and even show anger. This may understandably cause friends and family to feel insecure, as they may take this behavior quite personally. The result may be that those who wanted to keep company, console, and help, end up having less contact and visiting less often. This may cause the mourner to feel rejected while he grieves. The relative may not realize that in an emotional crisis, it is natural for the grieving person's responses to swing from one extreme to the other. It's important that those closest to the bereaved spouse not let his mood swings deter them from visiting again. Just like the mourner has to try to bear the tragedy that has befallen him, his family and friends must also try to tolerate the mourner while the worst runs its course. It is understandable that the grieving spouse should become self-centered in his grief at first. He may not realize that his own extreme responses are what discourage people from visiting him and cause them to withdraw. He may understand these things in context later on.

Many friends and relatives want to express their support by encouraging the grieving spouse and giving him advice. Sometimes they resort to something that has served a different mourner well. Suggestions may include going to a concert, taking up exercise, traveling abroad, and more. Many mourners find this sort of behavior overbearing. They often have no use for advice in the beginning and want to decide for themselves how they conduct their life at this time. A good rule of thumb may be to ask the grieving partner whether there is anything in particular that he wants to do or needs help with.

Many mourners may feel hurt and angry towards their relatives and friends who they expected to be more supportive after the loss. Mourners have a difficult time understanding why people might keep their distance, make little contact at first, or even almost vanish temporarily from the grieving spouse's life only to reappear as if nothing had happened. In such cases, it is difficult for the mourners to resume normal communication. Sometimes they wish not to have further contact with the person in question. They have been hurt by the person's behavior in this difficult time. When they had the greatest need for support they felt ignored and even rejected.

MORGAN AND VIVIAN

Morgan lost his wife Vivian after a short but difficult illness. They had three children, two of whom have left home. Morgan struggles to face the fact that Vivian is gone. He has isolated himself quite a bit, and it has become difficult for him to go out among people and be the odd one out among the other married couples in his circle of friends. Half a year after Vivian's death the group plans to meet at one couple's home, have dinner together, and schmooze over drinks like so often before. Morgan doesn't feel ready to go, but musters his courage at his friends' and children's encouragement and drives on over. His friends receive him well, embrace him and pat him on the shoulder, but nobody mentions Vivian, who had always been such a lively member of the group. Morgan expected someone to talk about her and would have appreciated it, but nobody says anything. He feels uncomfortable but tries to maintain a brave face. His discomfort increases dramatically when they sit down to dinner, and the chair across from him is empty. Morgan tries his best to participate in the dinnertime conversation. Everyone is sorry to see him go home straight after the meal, but Morgan doesn't have the energy to converse with his friends as they consume more and more red wine, all while seated across from Vivian's empty chair. He can't hold back the tears when he gets into his car.

CROSSING THE LINE

After the loss of a spouse, you may feel like you periodically need to decouple from social situations and be alone with yourself. This may be particularly strong in the first year, when you need time for yourself so you can allow yourself to release difficult emotions and pain. It is important to respect your own right to set limits for others under such circumstances. Even though you are fortunate in your nearest and dearest, this need for solitude can be strong, and it is important to respect it when it arises.

When the surviving spouse gradually begins to feel ready to go out and meet people more, at parties and events, he may feel he made the right decision because everything went well. He may feel that he should spend more time in social settings. On the other hand, other people's responses may sometimes surprise him. He had positive expectations and looked forward to seeing his friends, despite a certain anxiety and insecurity over entering a familiar setting alone this time. But when the moment comes, he may feel that friends and acquaintances who knew his spouse well avoid mentioning her name and act as if nothing has happened. The mourner may start asking questions. Have the friends forgotten his deceased spouse?

Sometimes the surviving spouse may have interactions with someone that are challenging. For example, he may find himself at a social gathering shortly after the loss and be approached by someone who has been drinking alcohol and tries insistently to discuss the deceased partner. This person wants to talk about what good friends they were, to reminisce about past events, and may even start tearing up while describing past experiences. The mourner, who is now trying to concentrate on handling a situation alone that he had usually handled with his spouse before, has no desire to discuss his late spouse with inebriated acquaintances. As a consequence, he may begin to avoid social gatherings where alcohol is served. Another example of behavior that crosses the line is when someone gets in touch soon after the spouse's passing in order to initiate a sexual relationship.

ALFRED AND JANE

Alfred is the CEO of a mid-size company. He lost his wife Jane after a three-year battle with cancer. Though Alfred knew quite clearly where things were headed, it came as a surprise to him how heavy a burden the grief was when it arrived. He thought he was relatively well prepared, he and his wife had spoken openly about what was to come, and he had bid his wife a heartfelt and sincere goodbye. After her passing, Alfred realizes that he will need a long time to recover from the loss. He feels the need to continue work and only wants to spend time with close friends and relatives, in addition to his children. This outgoing man finds that for the first time in his life, he needs to withdraw and spend time alone with himself. Three months after Jane's death, he gets a call from an old acquaintance, a woman, who wants to invite him over for dinner. This comes as quite a surprise, but he accepts the invitation, and they have an enjoyable evening. When the acquaintance keeps calling and wants to meet him again, he begins to suspect that she's after something more. When she calls him one night and propositions him, he is thoroughly offended and asks her to leave him alone. Alfred is surprised to see how many women begin to contact him and seek his company. He feels no desire for this, finds it pushy, and thinks it's much too soon after his wife's death.

III. TRANSITIONS

CHANGED CIRCUMSTANCES AFTER BEREAVEMENT

Spouses develop unique roles and communication patterns with each other. The patterns are usually clearer and more fixed in long relationships. Each partner's share in the responsibility for daily tasks like cooking, cleaning, finances, and car repair is often very clear. Where emotional matters are concerned, the pattern is often less clearly defined, but nevertheless it may become apparent upon close examination. One partner may be warmer, more communicative and more emotionally open; the other may be more comfortable giving praise, be the encouraging one, and have an easier time discussing sensitive issues and addressing tension. It often isn't until something special happens that people realize they've been living according to a certain pattern. It has gradually developed to the point of being relatively automatic, without the couple's having paid any particular attention to it. Many people have an easier time discerning the communication patterns of other couples than their own.

Upon losing a partner, the surviving partner must take on all the roles and begins to realize the importance of the other in his daily life. Our ability to handle new roles varies from person to person. Some have an easy time learning something new, while others may find it a great and even insurmountable task.

The loss of a spouse is also the loss of a certain status. Now you're just you. This changes your position both inward and outward, and it also affects how others see you and interact with you. You are in an altered role towards your children, whether young or grown. You are the only parent now. Your role toward your own family and your spouse's family also changes. Behavior, communication, and participation in various events and occasions with the family will not be the same as before.

Outwards, towards friends, your role is now different. You are no longer part of a "couple." You no longer have the role that "the two of you" played within the group. You may be invited for some things but not for others where you would have been included by default in the past. Sometimes you may find yourself excluded from something in a way that would never have occurred if your spouse were alive. You may also feel that you are spoken to in a different way from before.

Many find it difficult to face a changed position within their circle of friends and acquaintances after the loss. Going alone to a dinner party can be a stressful experience. It reminds you of the good old days when you were all together, and makes tangible the fact that you are now alone. Looking at the other couples and being alone yourself is an unpleasant reminder that your circumstances have changed and you no longer fit into your circle of friends because you're not part of a couple. It can also be painful to find out that old friends have gathered at someone's house, traveled abroad together, or gone out to dinner together without inviting you.

This changed position requires that you reexamine your roles and try to find new ones for yourself.

"We really should meet soon," they may
say and I suspect they don't mean it
and have a hard time pretending to believe them.
I'm pretty sure it's no longer high on these people's
wish lists to see me, I no longer fit into
their lives.

(*I Shall Not Want*)

SELF-IMAGE

Losing your spouse tests the strength of your self-image. Self-image refers to a person's consciousness of being distinct from other people, of being unique and unlike anyone else. People with a positive self-image have a good relationship with themselves and do not suffer from an inferiority complex. They are by and large satisfied with the kind of person they are, how they behave and how they communicate with others.

Those who have a negative self-image may struggle to differentiate themselves from others, often feel inferior and have negative feelings towards themselves. They are often indecisive communicators and allow others to walk over them. They are often too critical of themselves and interpret what happens in their life as being to their disadvantage. They are in the habit of thinking: "Trouble always seeks me out. This will never get better. I'll never get through." This way of thinking makes them more prone to being trapped in negative thoughts over the circumstances that now face them after losing a spouse. The way they think may make it more difficult to tackle grief and find a place in life after the loss. They are often dissatisfied with themselves, fear the judgment of others, adapt themselves too much to others' desires, and may have a tendency to blame others when things go badly.

Those who have a positive self-image have a stronger tendency to be optimistic, and their attitude toward life is more positive overall. Positive self-image can make it easier to find a way forward and search for new paths in changed circumstances.

It can be a great help for you, who have lost your spouse, to try to realize how your self-image, thoughts, and attitudes towards life affect your emotional state. If your self-image isn't strong enough, there is a risk that it will be severely threatened when a traumatic experience strikes. It is therefore very important for a person with a negative self-image to gradually try to strengthen it in order to be able to face life in a more positive way.

ATTITUDE TOWARDS SOLITUDE

Most people know the feeling of missing their partner under some temporary circumstances. This may have been an absence for work, an illness, or travel. As the separation wore on, the yearning for the spouse grew and became more palpable. When your spouse came back, the longing vanished and was replaced by relief and joy. The feeling of safety, that everything was alright again, just the way it should be, came instinctively.

It varies from person to person how we feel when we are alone. This is independent of whether or not we are in a relationship. People may become lonely after the loss of a spouse whether they have children or not. The loneliness may be far more acute, however, for those who have no children. How we handle solitude can be connected to earlier experiences. If the surviving spouse was raised in a peaceful and stable environment and learned to occupy himself as a child with work and play, he will likely be better equipped to handle solitude. Those who didn't receive this training as children may find themselves more anxious when loneliness comes calling.

Many people don't think particularly much about solitude until they lose their spouse. When solitude is temporary, there is no need to take a considered stance on it. When you have lost your spouse, however, this becomes a pressing need. Solitude cannot be escaped anymore, it has found its way into life whether you wanted it to or not. The surviving spouse is often alone now and must seek to bear the solitude. If he cannot tolerate being alone, that may cause a special sense of loneliness that is an unfamiliar emotion to him.

The ability of the surviving spouse to be self-sufficient will gradually be put to the test. He must now sleep alone, and cook only for himself. Just these two points are striking examples of the transformation of his personal circumstances.

When you lose your spouse, it is important to try to develop coping mechanisms and a positive disposition towards solitude. You must try to learn gradually to enjoy being alone with yourself, be patient and tolerant, to like yourself and take pleasure in your own company. Try to find your own balance, and also try to enjoy other people's company. You may find you have to make an effort to be active and engaged – it won't happen of its own accord.

FEELING GOOD IN YOUR OWN COMPANY

It is important for you to try to enjoy the moment again when you find yourself alone. Try to notice and take joy in the little things in life, like the way leaves move in a breeze, the smell of flowers, or the way your body moves when you walk. Allow yourself to be curious and feel wonder at the little things in life and what you are aware of from moment to moment.

Also allow yourself to relax with a book, some music, or a good movie. This will give you peace of mind for a while and should help you to become gradually more comfortable in your own company. It is important not to give up on difficult days when tears overpower you. Allow yourself to cry, as it is a relief and a part of your grief processing. You will usually feel better after a good cry, and you will feel more intimately and deeply in touch with yourself. Don't give up. Try to harness the power within yourself and enjoy life in your own special ways. Try to make patience, courage and endurance your friends in the grieving process.

IV. PARENTING AND THE LOSS OF A SPOUSE

WHAT WILL BECOME OF ME?

Many bereaved partners become filled with insecurity over the future and the tasks of the present day. The feeling of "What will become of me?" can be oppressive in the first few days. Questions like "How will I get through this alone?" or "Can I handle all our joint obligations on my own?" are not uncommon, especially where children are concerned. People feel like their feet have been pulled out from under them. Plans for the future will change and be disturbed significantly.

It may be a source of increased stress to feel uncertain about your economic situation and have to consider changes to your family circumstances. Finances are a common source of anxiety in the wake of a loss, especially if your late spouse was the primary breadwinner. In the immediate aftermath of the loss, it is important to avoid making major decisions about the future, if at all possible. Once a bit more balance is attained and your mind is calmer, it is more likely that your decisions will be made with deliberation and in accordance with your true wishes.

Many people who lose their spouse have children. Some have young children, others have older ones who still need a great deal of care and affection. One who has lost his partner may therefore be in the difficult position of having to console and support his children while he himself is shattered with grief. This is a complicated role, as the parent must embrace himself while fulfilling his role as next of kin for his children, who have lost their other parent. Often there is more than one child, their ages differ, and they need different kinds of support.

Under these circumstances, the parent must have great stamina and try to understand each child's emotional life in order to meet her or his unique needs. Upon the loss of a spouse, the parent suddenly bears sole responsibility for all aspects of the family's life, including childrearing. The parent may feel obligated to perform well every day and always be there for the children. This change in circumstances may force the survivor to set aside many of his own needs in order to be there for the children. This can be a source of considerable stress in the parent's life, and this responsibility can be almost overpowering in some cases.

Your sympathy with the children may be very strong, informed by a powerful understanding of how much they have lost and how much they miss their parent. The surviving parent may wonder whether the children will receive all the love and care they need from now on. Many parents feel a real anxiety in the wake of their spouse's death, centered on their ability to provide for their children and the future that awaits them. You may grapple with thoughts about whether you can provide your children with good living conditions or whether they will live a life of deprivation, something you had never expected or intended. What about supporting them through school? Questions and anxieties about your finances and your children's future are very common.

The children's grief can increase the grief and insecurity of the parents. At the same time, the parent experiences deep joy and gratitude over having children. They give a fullness to life; they are the future. Bearing sole responsibility for children increases the parent's consciousness that nothing serious must happen to him. Nothing must threaten the children's safety and stability beyond what is already done. By the same token, the parent may feel that his own importance has increased dramatically, and this may be a source of strength going forward.

It is not uncommon for a family where one parent has passed away to have to change living circumstances, for instance by moving to a different apartment. A long workday and the absences it requires from the home may be a source of stress. The children may not get the time they need with their parent.

JULIA AND DAVID

Julia has just been widowed. She is thirty-seven years old. Her husband had sustained grave injuries in an accident at work and died three months later. They had two children, Maria, age nine, and Ross, who was four. Julia was an educated social worker, but hadn't worked outside the home since Ross was born. Her husband, David, was the love of her life. He was twelve years her senior. They knew from the start that they were meant for each other, and the relationship had always been intimate and rewarding. Julia received considerable insurance payments after her loss, which helped ease her finances and her worries about making ends meet at first.

Julia has good friends who helped her take care of the children in the early days. When Julia thinks back to that difficult time, a few years later, she feels an enduring gratitude for the support she received during that difficult time.

Despite this help, the parenting role was a considerable strain for Julia. One particular incident haunts her memory: she was alone with the children when Ross had a major temper tantrum, and she herself retreated to her bedroom to cry, overpowered by grief and her inability to manage the situation. In her mind's eye, she can see her daughter Maria's face as she looks on from a distance. Then Maria walks silently into her bedroom and shuts the door. After the children had fallen asleep, Julia cried over their beds. For years she felt guilty over sometimes being irritated with the children and not supporting them like she should have. But gradually Julia has been able to forgive herself after seeking professional assistance and realizing that her behavior was normal and she was just trying to do her best.

UNDERSTANDING CHILDREN'S EMOTIONAL STATES

It may be useful to a surviving parent to know a few fundamentals about children's grief responses. Knowledge about children and their grief is just as important for parents as knowledge of their own responses. Knowing what is considered a normal range of responses for a child can reduce the strain on the parent.

Children grieve like adults; it has been demonstrated that their grieving process obeys similar laws. The manifestations of grief in children, however, depend on their age and maturity. The intellectual maturity of a child exerts a strong influence on how she grieves. A child's emotional bond with the deceased parent also affects the response. It is generally believed that children are more likely to shut out their grief than adults, and they often make an effort to hide it. This is not least true of older children and teenagers, who try to hide their grief in order to spare their parent. They are perfectly well aware of their parent's suffering.

FIRST REACTIONS

Each child responds to a traumatic event in his own way. This reaction will depend on whether the parent passed away suddenly or there was time to prepare the child for the loss. If the parent had been ill for a long time and the child was kept informed about the illness and its seriousness, she may have been better prepared emotionally when the sick parent passed away. Such information can help a child to face grief and soften the first reaction. Yet, however well prepared for the shock, children usually show common *first* responses to grief:

- Shock and denial
- Fear and protestation
- Numbness and paralysis
- Pretending that nothing has happened

SHOCK AND DENIAL

When children are informed of the death of a parent, it is common for them to question the veracity of the report. They may say, "That's not right" or "That's not true," as well as "You must have misunderstood." Such reactions are more common among older children and teens. When the shock strikes, they deny the facts and don't show much emotion at first. They try to keep the pain away for a time. Disbelief and denial in the early stages protects the child from being overpowered with emotion. When a child shows little or no emotional response at first, the parent may worry that the child doesn't cry more and doesn't express more clearly how she feels. Such a response indicates that the child is absorbing what has happened, step by step. Under normal circumstances, the child will gradually face the facts and show more adequate grief responses.

FEAR AND PROTESTATION

Some children react very strongly to a parent's death and immediately show symptoms of great fear. They may cry unconsolably and protest against what has happened. They may feel terrified about what will happen to them and fear losing their other parent as well. A child in this situation needs a great deal of affection and support, and this will require time and attention from the surviving parent. If the parent can respond to this need, the child will grow calmer and feel more secure.

NUMBNESS AND PARALYSIS

A child may act very distant and seem almost paralyzed after he receives the news of his parent's death. He may be unresponsive. The child may stop playing; the engagement and joy that used to characterize her games may vanish. Such numbness may last from a few hours to several days, or even longer.

PRETENDING THAT NOTHING HAPPENED

Sometimes a child receives the news that his parent has passed away and listens attentively to information about the death. Afterwards, however, the child may act as if nothing has happened and want to go back out to play or do whatever he was doing before the news arrived. Reactions of this kind do not mean that the child didn't love the late parent. Rather, they show that she wants to keep difficult emotions away for a while. The child tries to distract herself and focus her attentions on something else in order to soften the pain.

When the response takes this form, it is important to help the child absorb the fact of the death by discussing it slowly and talking about what has happened. Approaching the child may be quite the balancing act, and it will also take time. In most cases, the child will come to terms with what has happened and transition gradually to a normal emotional response.

CHILDREN OF DIFFERENT AGES

TWO-FIVE YEARS OLD

At this age, children are self-centered and often think that what has happened is somehow their fault. They may think someone else has disappeared or died because of them. Children of pre-school age usually don't understand the finality of death and therefore don't respond strongly at first. They also find it difficult to describe complicated emotions.

FIVE-TEN YEARS OLD

At this age, children gradually gain increased understanding that death is final and irrevocable. Their emotional responses and grief are therefore stronger.

TEN AND OLDER

From ten years of age, children's ideas about death become more complex and realistic. They may become preoccupied with questions about life and death, justice and injustice, as well as wanting to discuss the supernatural.

COMMON GRIEF RESPONSES IN CHILDREN

The grief of losing a parent and the instability and changes that follow can have serious consequences for the child. These consequences may also manifest themselves later in life. In this context, the possibility of depression in adulthood is a common concern. It is therefore important to try to understand children's grief and help them as much as possible to handle difficult and painful emotions. When the child has processed his grief, it is important to help him express himself so he can find release for his imaginings and emotions. It is important to give the child a chance to see and say goodbye to the deceased parent. The surviving parent should not hide his grief from the child unless his reactions are so strong that he risks losing control. It can be good for a child to see that it is normal to grieve, to be sad and down, and that it is possible to talk about missing someone and about difficult emotions. This sends the child the message that it's alright to express yourself and grieve.

If the grief is so hard for the child that the parent feels unable to help, professional assistance should be sought. This may include situations where the parent observes major changes in the child's behavior or where the child seems trapped in his grief.

Common *grief* responses in children after a traumatic loss can include:

- Anxiety
- Haunting memories
- Sleep disturbances
- Sadness and longing
- Anger and attention-seeking
- Guilt and self-blaming
- Difficulties in school
- Physical symptoms

ANXIETY

Upon losing a parent, the child's security is seriously threatened. Anxiety is one of the most common responses that children show when they lose a parent. When one parent dies, the other might die as well. This fact can cause such overwhelming anxiety that it fills the minds of many children. Children are often more afraid that something will happen to their surviving parent than that something will happen to themselves.

The manifestation of anxiety depends on the child's age. Small children can become demanding, experience separation anxiety and often don't want to let their parent out of sight. Children may seek security in various ways, for instance not wanting to be home alone, not wanting to sleep elsewhere, or wanting to sleep with the lights on. An older child may develop a phobia toward something, particularly if the death occurred suddenly, if the child witnessed an accident, or perhaps even was the one to find the deceased parent. They won't want to talk about what happened and avoid all memories of the event. Such responses serve the purpose of protecting the child from strong emotional responses.

It is also often observed that children behave as if they're on alert after a loss. They are constantly on guard and may jump at the slightest provocation. This may cause increased tension and produce physical symptoms like muscular tension, stomach pains and headaches.

HAUNTING MEMORIES

Haunting memories may be "seared" into a child's mind. If the child witnessed an accident or a shocking event, the memories may be preserved like an "internal video recording" in the child's mind. These images emerge later and haunt them. Precise details of sound, smell, or touch can be embedded in the child's consciousness and be hard to break free from. They may disturb sleep and cause malaise, in addition to affecting dreams and nightmares.

SLEEP DISTURBANCES

Children who have lost a parent often have trouble sleeping. They may find it difficult to fall asleep and wake up in the middle of the night. This may be connected to the use of the word "to fall asleep" in relation to death, and the child may be afraid to fall asleep. Sleep disturbances may also be caused by thoughts of the deceased parent and death that haunt the child around bedtime. The anxiety that results from these thoughts makes sleeping even more difficult.

Some children may wake up from bad dreams or nightmares. They don't want to go to sleep for fear that they will have bad dreams. This may give rise to a need to sleep in bed with a parent or sibling. Experience shows that children who don't have an opportunity to process grief and express themselves about it have worse dreams and more frequent nightmares than other children.

SADNESS AND LONGING

Sadness and longing for the lost parent can manifest themselves in various ways in children. Some cry a great deal and can be nearly inconsolable, others cry less and are sad for a shorter time. This is particularly true of small children. Regression to previous developmental states is common for children in the immediate wake of a parent's death. A child who has stopped using a pacifier may want it again. A child who has stopped wetting the bed may start doing so again. An older child may want a hug more often and to curl up in her parent's embrace, something she rarely sought after before. These are all natural responses that help the child recover and regain his sense of security.

Sometimes sadness and longing for the parent manifest in the child's being withdrawn and wanting to isolate herself. Many children become more closed than they were before and express themselves less. This is particularly true of older children. They often become preoccupied with trying to protect their parent from further difficulties.

A situation like this may last a long time for a child who has lost a parent. The child dwells at length on memories of the parent, perhaps even feels the parent's presence, and tries to act like the parent used to. The longing for the parent is strong. Sometimes, the child may also feel a certain sense of relief after the loss, perhaps if the parent had been very ill or if parent and child had a complicated relationship. If this is the case, the child may be faced with very complex and contradictory feelings, and it is important to try to understand the child's position and help her.

ANGER AND ATTENTION-SEEKING

A child may show great anger and have a great need for attention after losing a parent. The anger often emerges direct and unrestrained through hitting, kicking, and screaming. The child may say things like "Daddy was so stupid to drive like an idiot." Anger may take various forms and have different targets. Children frequently direct their anger at:

- Death – for taking the parent
- God – for allowing it to happen
- Adults – for not letting the child participate in their grief
- Someone else – for not having prevented the death
- Themselves – for failing to prevent what happened
- The deceased parent – for having betrayed or abandoned them

Expressions of anger are often connected to the child's need for more attention. The child shows anger in order to get the parent to take better care of them and be more attentive to them. It can be stressful for the parent when children are very angry. Anger is a natural emotion. It may be necessary to take some time to discuss anger especially with the children. This can help them to express themselves and channel their anger in ways that are harmless both to themselves and others.

GUILT AND SELF-BLAMING

Children may believe that they are somehow responsible for a parent's death. They may believe that their own thoughts, emotions, and behaviors were partially the cause of what happened. They blame themselves. As mentioned before, this response is more common when children's thinking is still self-centered. They then often overestimate their own influence over external events. School-age children and teenagers can also blame themselves, even though they are no longer as self-centered. A boy who lost his mother at age eleven and received psychological counseling as a sixteen-year-old turned out to have blamed himself for being difficult to his mother. A girl who lost her mother to suicide at age four told a counselor when she was eleven that she could remember thinking at the time that if she had tidied her room better her mom wouldn't have died.

Guilt and self-blaming can also emerge if the relationship with the deceased parent was difficult. The child often regrets not having been kinder to the parent and feels bad that his behavior was sometimes the cause of arguments. The child may also feel regret over not having expressed more love and affection for the deceased parent.

DIFFICULTIES IN SCHOOL

Children's grief can affect their schoolwork. This most often presents as difficulty paying attention and concentrating. Thoughts and memories of what has happened, as well as anxiety and worries about family matters, are a prominent presence in the child's mind. The grief and sadness cause them to think more slowly, and their energy and strength are diminished. The child may struggle to complete an assignment and feel it's too difficult. When asked to read aloud, the child may not know where to start, and when called upon to answer a question, she may be completely lost. Sometimes the child's feelings and experiences may be expressed quite directly through schoolwork, for instance in drawings and writing assignments. A child who used to be active and engaged and participated in social activities may now be apathetic, inactive, and unwilling to participate with other children. The child may choose to isolate herself and be alone.

It often turns out that a child who used to perform very well in school no longer does so. Grades slip and overall engagement with school activities decreases. Difficulties with school after losing a parent occur regardless of the child's level in school. Though many of the symptoms of grief after losing a parent disappear gradually, difficulties at school can last for a long time, even several years. This has raised many school principals' and teachers' awareness of children's grieving process.

PHYSICAL SYMPTOMS

Grieving children often develop physical symptoms like headaches, stomach aches, and muscular pains. Adults often pay a great deal of attention to these complaints and they may cause the surviving parent to worry. The child can feel that he receives increased attention from the parent and other adults when he feels bad and may try to use these symptoms to get more care and attention from the adults. It is important not to belittle children's physical symptoms but to bear in mind that they may be a manifestation of emotional pain. If a child appears to be getting stuck in a pattern of complaining about physical discomforts, it is advisable to seek professional assistance.

BOYS AND GIRLS IN GRIEF

There can be a considerable difference between how boys and girls respond to grief. Boys usually have a more difficult time than girls with expressing their emotions and putting memories into words. Boys are less likely to process grief through conversation. On the other hand, boys are known to express grief through anger more often than girls. Girls generally seem to utilize sources of support in the environment more often than boys; they talk about grief both at home and to friends. Grieving boys more often seek release through activity and enterprise.

The gender difference in response becomes more evident with age. It is observed among young school-age children but becomes more apparent among teenagers.

New long-term studies seem to show, contrary to what was previously believed, that the loss of a parent can be worse for girls than for boys in the long run. (*Journal of the Norwegian Association of Psychologists*) They seem to be more susceptible to depression as adults and develop more serious psychological consequences than boys. This is quite surprising, especially in light of what was already mentioned about the gender difference in articulation of grief. There may be many different factors at play here. For instance, girls may be more emotionally aware, paying more attention to others' feelings and interpersonal relationships. Girls are often more sensitive to tension within families. They are prone to worry if something is wrong. Boys are more outward-seeking. They seem to have an easier time keeping emotions at a distance and looking on down the road. It has been pointed out that the methods that have been developed to help children through grief have centered more on girls than boys, thanks to a greater emphasis on emotional matters in the grieving process. Boys may benefit more from being able to work with their experiences and grief through a variety of activities.

There may thus be no reason to fear if boys express themselves verbally less than girls. Verbal expression may simply not be their way to process grief. Yet there is reason to pay attention if boys withdraw from their usual activities, change their behavior, and neglect school activities. This may be a reason for parents to worry and seek professional help.

PRACTICAL ADVICE FOR PARENTS

It is a challenge for a parent to place himself in the shoes of a child who has lost her other parent. The surviving parent has to give the child security, support, and warmth without being overprotective. Much is at stake for a child in being able to rely on the parent's support even as the parent himself struggles with grief. The parent has to separate his grief from the child's grief and support the child when needed. In turn, the parent must seek others' support in his own grief.

The following points are conceived as guidelines for parents who are helping children with grief processing.

OPEN AND HONEST DISCUSSIONS

- Give explanations that suit the child's developmental level.
- Avoid complicated explanations.
- Eliminate uncertainty and send a clear message.

- Tell the child about the death immediately and give her correct information about what happened.
- Do not use words like "trip" or "sleep" to describe death.
- Tell the child that the parent will not come back.

MAKE THE LOSS REAL

- Talk to the child about your community's funeral rites and what happens to the body.
- Allow the child to see the deceased parent, if possible.
- Allow the child to participate in the funeral, if possible.
- If there is a grave or memorial, take the child there and enlist his help in maintaining the grave.
- Maintain the memory of the parent by talking about them and looking at family photographs.
- Don't hide your own grief from the child unless absolutely necessary.

PROCESS PROBLEMS

- Allow discussion and questions.
- Keep conversations short, as children often don't have much stamina.
- Answer the same questions again and again and repeat the sequence of events to the child when asked.

- Listen attentively to the child and encourage it to express itself, but try not to push too much.

DIMINISH FEAR AND GUILT

- Talk to the child about how natural it is to be afraid in these circumstances.
- Tell the child that the surviving parent will do everything possible to help the child to feel better.
- Explain to the child that it is very unlikely that the surviving parent will die and be taken from her.
- Convince the child that the parent's death was not her fault.

Other factors can be important, too, such as making sure that a child can stay in the same daycare center or school, if possible. It is important to inform the school or daycare center about the child's situation and emotional state. It can be a great support to the child if daily life can be kept as unchanged as possible. Try to prevent relocation and changes in environment at first.

It is worth reiterating that if the grief proves very burdensome for the child, it is important to get outside help and possibly individual therapy. This is not least to prevent difficulties that may arise later in life.

Most of all, I want Jai to be happy in the years ahead. So if she finds happiness through remarriage, that will be great. If she finds happiness without remarrying, that will also be great.

(*The Last Lecture*)

A NEW RELATIONSHIP AFTER THE LOSS

Many wonder when it is advisable to start a new relationship after losing your spouse. There are no hard and fast rules in these matters. People who have lost a spouse are different individuals with different needs, and their ages and situations in life can vary greatly. Some have had a long build-up to the loss, while others are bereaved quite suddenly. If the bereaved partner has not been able to let his late spouse go and process his grief well enough, it can be complicated for him to connect to a new person. He may experience tension over being in a new relationship, loving and enjoying, but simultaneously feeling sadness and grief over the lost spouse.

To start a new relationship, an individual must be capable of giving, receiving, and enjoying, and must not be too preoccupied with the past.

It is a cause for joy in and of itself when those who have lost their spouse find a new life partner. Most adults want to be in an intimate relationship with another person whom they can share life with. The desire for love, intimacy, and a sexual connection is strong and natural. The need for a new relationship may thus be great, both among young people and those in middle age. They often have a strong sex drive and are understandably drawn to a new relationship. On the other hand, older individuals who have grown children and grandchildren are often more focused on their relationships with them.

When the surviving spouse has children, starting a new relationship can be a sensitive affair. Many children find it difficult to see their parent in a new relationship. This is especially true of older kids and teens. There may be direct resistance towards this new individual. Great conflict and unhappiness often emerge in conjunction with this. Children may experience the surviving parent's new relationship as a betrayal of the deceased parent. Children may also feel guilty if they begin to care about someone other than the parent they lost.

It is often difficult for the adults involved when children gain a step-parent. This situation requires the new spouse to show the children particular care and sensitivity and to try to understand their situation. If both partners have children, the new relationship will be even more complex.

Competition between the children for love, attention, and affection may result. The children may also feel jealousy and anger. But then again, communication often goes well, even better than the adults dared to hope. The children then adapt to each other gradually and gain new playmates and friends.

A FEW POINTS FOR CONSIDERATION

All sorts of issues may arise in the surviving partner's mind as he considers entering a new relationship. Those listed here are just a small sample, by no means exhaustive but intended to provoke further reflection.

- How will the spouse's own family (parents, siblings, etc.) respond to the new spouse?
- How will the former in-laws respond to the new partner?
- How will the new relationship affect communication with friends and family?
- Do any steps need to be taken with regard to finances and inheritance matters?
- Will it be necessary to change living circumstances?

V. REACTION PATTERNS

GENDER DIFFERENCES

From early childhood, you can see differences in reaction patterns between the genders. These differences are related to personal, social, and gender-related development. Many cultures have a tendency to place less emphasis on physical and emotional closeness when raising boys than girls. Intimacy, bonding, and personal communication are far more characteristic of the upbringing and communication patterns of girls. This childhood influence lasts into adulthood, and the genders tend to express themselves in somewhat different ways when it comes to emotional matters.

When discussing differences in men's and women's emotional responses, it is important to bear in mind that not all men follow a single pattern, nor all women. Some men tend to react in ways more commonly associated with women and vice versa, as we will touch on later.

Men have a certain tendency to express their emotions less than women. Men often try to avoid conflict. They can become evasive and withdrawn when emotional issues are under discussion. Men are more often inclined toward looking for resolution and action than conversation. They may even use silence deliberately when matters of conflict are on the table, unlike women.

Another difference is that women tend to be more concerned with appealing to other people. They place a greater emphasis on bonding with others and often have a tendency to take responsibility for other people's emotional states.

It can be challenging for men to deal with emotional matters if they are closed and struggle with expressing themselves. They not only struggle to talk to their spouses about their feelings, but often they don't talk about personal matters with male friends, either. When asked whether they share their personal lives with their friends, most men answer that they don't.

THE SHAPING OF BOYS AND GIRLS

In order to understand better how women's and men's responses differ, it is essential to realize that many factors, such as upbringing, family relationships, genetics, and social structure, are all important. *(In the Prime of Life.)*

Our gender identity is one of the most profound feelings we have about ourselves. As early as about three years of age, a child begins to feel that it belongs to a certain gender. Though girls and boys play together, their participation in activities quickly differentiates itself according to gender, and they increasingly choose different activities and games as they grow older. Boys and girls differentiate themselves most clearly at the age of about seven to twelve.

It is necessary for a child to connect deeply and intimately with her parent and to trust him or her implicitly. Sometimes a child is in symbiosis with the parent, a situation in which the child doesn't separate itself from the parent. Beginning at an early age, boys become gradually more aware of their gender and receive the message that they are different from their mothers and should behave differently from how they do. They are encouraged to be assertive and physically active. A girl has her primary parental figure, most often her mother, as a role model growing up. She therefore doesn't receive the message that she should differentiate herself from her mother, but rather that she should imitate her in speech and behavior. She gradually transfers these behaviors and attitudes to other relationships she forms, including with other girls, but also with adults outside the family. Her self-image becomes very strongly connected with and dependent on the relationships she forms with others. She gets recognition for being able to show others empathy and for being understanding. She doesn't learn to set clear boundaries and differentiate herself from others to the same extent. Girls and boys thus receive praise for different personal approaches and behaviors in interpersonal relationships.

WOMEN AND MEN IN GRIEF

Women and men often face grief in different ways. Men often repress their grief and are closed in their bereavement. That is a major reason why they are often affected worse by traumatic events than women. Men are less likely to seek help from friends or professionals.

Men frequently try to process their grief by finding something to do and staying active. Women commonly give their emotions and feelings more space. Men describe feeling unable to articulate their feelings in the face of adversity. It can be a struggle to put things into words. On the other hand, emotional pain can take such a powerful hold on women that they struggle to keep going with their lives. Women often have an easier time talking about their emotions. They share their grief with others in a more open and sincere manner and are less likely to hide it. Their reactions are often opposite to those of men, who often seem to be calm and collected. These behaviors are often interpreted to indicate that the man doesn't care much, that he is unemotional and hard.

THE MALE MODEL AND THE FEMALE MODEL

"Some scholars such as Dr. Phyllis Silverman have advanced the idea that the genders' grief responses can be classified according to two models, the 'male model' and the 'female model.' Though the models are differentiated based on gender, not all men follow the 'male model,' nor all women the 'female model.' Silverman points out that those who fall under the 'male model' try to distance themselves from the past. They want to 'get on with their lives' and be independent. They also emphasize work and try to avoid losing control around others.

"Those who fall under the 'female model,' on the other hand, emphasize communication and emotional connectedness. Those who follow this pattern agree with statements like 'You don't sever your ties with the past, you change them' and tend to grieve more visibly, to seek help and to discuss their grief more openly.

"In this context, it is important to appreciate that both women and men grieve in ways that are consistent with how they respond overall to life events. Irrespective of which model we follow, the purpose is to re-adapt to life. That is normal grief processing."

(Silverman, P., quoted in Neeld, G.H. article http://www.connect.legacy.com)

INTERACTING WITH GRIEVING MEN AND WOMEN

There are a few points that it may be useful to keep in mind when interacting with people who are grieving. When they receive recognition that their grief reactions are neither right nor wrong, they feel understood and experience empathy. Women have a right to react like they do and men have the same right to respond to grief in their own way. The genders can learn from each other, however, and can support each other by respecting both approaches and resisting the tendency to pressure others to grieve in ways that don't feel normal to them.

He:

- Don't expect tears, but understand that his emotions are strong.
- Don't expect him to express his emotions.
- Be prepared for him to want to solve problems in an intellectual way and look for solutions. This is his way to understand the loss and face a new life.
- Recognize and respect his need for peace and solitude. This is not a rejection of support, but rather an expression of the need for independence and self-control in grief.
- Recognize and respect his need to focus his energies on the future rather than the past. This is his way of adapting to life again.

She:

- Expect many tears; they are natural and healthy. Don't encourage her to hold them back.
- Acknowledge her need to share and discuss the loss; this may be a source of comfort to her. This is not a search for answers, but a way to understand the loss and face a new life.
- Recognize and respect her need for support from outside her immediate family. She is not rejecting the support that is already available, but rather satisfying her need for social interactions.
- Acknowledge and respect her need to focus her energies on the past. This is her way of maintaining a connection with her lost loved one.

WHEN A LOSS IS NOT JUST A LOSS

When you have had a good relationship, it usually proves easier to say goodbye to your spouse. If on the other hand the relationship was characterized by tension and long-term conflict, the loss can be very difficult. The circumstances surrounding the loss can sometimes be very complex, and this can also affect the grieving process. A few examples include: When the surviving partner discovers something problematic about her spouse just before or after the loss; when the death was a suicide, an accident, or inflicted by another person; when a natural disaster, a disappearance, or suspicious circumstances surround the death; and when the partners had tried for years to have a child but one spouse passes away before this wish can be fulfilled. It is further worth mentioning the possible complications that might arise if the surviving partner has stepchildren. In many such cases, people must not only handle the grief of losing the spouse, but are forced to do so while their mind is occupied with other, unexpected negative emotions. This might be termed a twofold trauma, which entails additional stress and greater inner conflict.

PETER AND STEPHANIE

Peter and Stephanie have just celebrated their silver wedding anniversary. One evening when Stephanie is away from home, Peter sees a message for her in the computer. A closer look reveals that she has been having an affair with another man for two years, without Peter's suspecting a thing. A week later, Stephanie dies in a car crash. Her death is doubly traumatic for Peter. Now he has to deal not only with the loss of his wife, but also the complex set of feelings connected with her infidelity and the dilemma of whether or not to share that knowledge with his children.

BLAIR AND ALEX

Blair and Alex are both divorced when they meet. They are in middle age and each has two children from a prior marriage. They fall deeply in love and feel they have finally found the love of their lives. They move in together and marry soon thereafter. Blair is fairly well off financially when they meet, but Alex is not. Blair is thus able to invest a substantial amount of money in their shared home. A few months after the wedding, Alex is revealed to be seriously ill with cancer. He dies seven months later. Blair is knocked completely off her feet. She feels she'll never recover from the loss. Soon after Alex's death, his children begin to demand their paternal inheritance. Blair feels utterly unable to deal with this issue so soon. Alex's children won't back down and put a great deal of pressure on Blair. She has to escape the strain, and with the help of good friends she decides to divide up her property as soon as possible. She can't understand how people can behave this way at such a sensitive time and feels anger growing within her. Her anger is directed at the behavior of the children, who believe they now have a right to the money that she alone earned and invested in the home she and Alex shared.

COMPLICATED GRIEF

Most people deal with grief temporarily – at first through painful longing, numbness, even guilt and anger. The surviving spouse gradually accepts the loss and moves on, often under changed premises and with a new perspective on life.

For some, however, the grief persists almost unchanged from the immediate aftermath of the spouse's death. This is called complicated grief. When grief is complicated, it is accompanied by so much pain and lasts so long that it prevents the surviving spouse from recognizing the loss and living a normal life. It is not known exactly why this happens, but aspects such as personality traits, genetic factors and unusual circumstances surrounding bereavement seem to play an important role.

Complicated grief not only affects the surviving spouse's quality of life and communication with family and friends, but can also have a direct impact on physical health. It is critical for those dealing with complicated grief to seek professional assistance.

OSCAR AND HELEN

Oscar is sixty-two years old. He lost his wife, Helen, in a car accident six years ago. They have three adult daughters and had lost their son to leukemia when he was eight years old. The eldest of their daughters was newly married when Helen died. She now has two children, two and four years old, and they are Oscar's only grandchildren. Oscar, who is an engineer with a private business, cannot work for three months after his wife's death but then has to return to work, as projects are piling up. When a year has passed after Helen's death, Oscar's life has returned to a regular routine. He takes care of his everyday tasks, but although he used to be social and extroverted, he is less socially engaged and his life revolves more and more exclusively around work. He spends most of his free time at home. After losing Helen, Oscar often thinks back to the time when they lost their son and remembers how much they supported each other in their grief. They were able to find a way forward because they had each other and could talk so intimately about everything that had happened – but now he has only himself.

The family stands close together and supports each other after Helen's death, but gradually the time Oscar spends with his daughters decreases. He visits them less often and spends less and less time with his grandchildren. When he comes to dinner with his daughter and her family, he shows no interest in the children but wants to sit with his daughter and discuss her mother, often reminiscing about the accident and its circumstances. The daughter has been worried for quite some time about her father's prolonged sadness and has, along with her younger sisters, encouraged him to rejoin his local Lions Club and reconnect with old friends, who have been calling him, visiting him, and trying unsuccessfully to get him to visit them. People gradually give up on encouraging him. Though several years have passed since Helen's death, not much has changed for Oscar. He wants to spend most of his time alone, is depressed, and has little ability to connect with others. He's gained weight and his daughters worry that he drinks too much. When five years have passed, the daughters join forces and meet with their father to tell him that something has to change. The eldest daughter is angry and says her father shows no interest in his grandchildren and is oblivious to the fact that they miss him. They are forced to watch him waste his life away. Oscar replies that he has nothing to live for since his wife died. He often wants to die himself. This arouses both anger and sympathy in his daughters. They have often discussed the possibility of getting outside help for their father, but now they insist that he seek assistance. They point out that he has been in a state of misery for way too long and that he seems unable to find a way out himself. There are no indications that anything is going to change, and he seems just as grief-stricken now as he did just after their mother died. They are able to convince their father that he needs professional help because he is in a completely awful state, and they are glad and relieved that he is willing to face himself and his grief with others' help.

SYMPTOMS OF COMPLICATED GRIEF

- Constant preoccupation with the loss and memories of the lost loved one
- An overpowering longing for the spouse
- Difficulty acknowledging the fact that the loss is permanent
- Numbness and indifference
- Bitterness over the loss
- A reduced capacity to enjoy life

- Depression and profound unhappiness
- Difficulty handling daily life
- Social isolation
- Lack of purpose
- Irritation and restlessness
- Mistrust of others

VI. FROM GRIEF TO COMPASSION

CARRY ME

Carry me across depths where I cannot touch bottom.
Lift me over obstacles that seem too tall.
Hold me tight
so I don't lose my way.
You who caused me to be born,
help me now to live.

(The Prayer Book)

SELF-COMPASSION

Nobody wants to feel unhappy. Most people try to find balance again when their emotional or physical equilibrium is disturbed. Many think at first after the loss of a spouse that they will never feel better, that unhappiness is here to stay. People may ask themselves questions like „Will I ever be normal again?" It's hardly an effective solution to tell yourself „Stop making yourself feel bad, this will get better." This will not release the pain. It doesn't vanish on command, or because we try to think of or do something else. At first, sorrow won't take any orders from the mind.

It is important that we respect our own feelings and emotions, that we realize we have every right to them, no matter what they may be. We are allowed to feel the way we feel. The first steps back to equilibrium are the recognition of how we feel and the gradual discovery of how we can begin to feel better.

EMOTIONS ARE MESSENGERS

Emotions are neither right nor wrong. They are messengers, and the messages they deliver deserve our attention. It is not right to delegitimize emotions by looking at them as unwise or illogical. Emotions inform us about our own state of being, and we should allow ourselves to experience them in full depth. Emotions just are. They are always genuine and true.

How well people are in touch with their innermost emotions varies. The loss of a spouse challenges us to articulate sensitive and personal feelings and put them into words. In this context, it can be important to reflect on whether you are emotionally open or closed. For instance, are you only open when everything is alright and you feel fine, but shut down and close your feelings inside when you're in turmoil and off balance? Or do you follow some different pattern?

Many are faced with a shortage of words and a lack of experience when it comes to emotional matters. They have few words to describe their feelings, but experience pain and suffering nevertheless. When you are able to put your pain and suffering into words, it may be easier to cry, and crying in turn releases tension and reduces stress. Feeling compassion for yourself and trying to improve your skills in the expression of emotions can be a critical step forward in the grieving process.

It is difficult to direct emotions. They come and go and are often overwhelming and confusing. Recognizing your emotions, discussing them with others, trying to disentangle them, and developing your ability to remain at peace are critical elements of dealing with the loss of a spouse and can determine whether we can take joy in and enjoy life again.

Feeling self-compassion is a valuable strategy to calm the emotions and to give yourself more control over how you feel.

EVERYONE DESERVES COMPASSION

Showing yourself compassion is not so different from being compassionate toward others, except that the compassion is now directed inwards. Reflect for a moment on what it feels like to show someone else compassion. You can show someone else compassion by being aware of the fact that they don't feel well. You can also show someone compassion when you know they have been through a difficult time or had a traumatic experience, and you realize how bad he or she feels. The suffering of your fellow human being touches you so you are prepared to share that suffering with them. You sympathize with them. You put yourself in their shoes. You can even imagine being in their circumstances. This is how you show them compassion. It often takes patience and endurance to develop your compassionate side. Compassion also means that you make an effort to show understanding and friendship when someone else reacts in a certain way or makes a mistake, instead of being harsh and condemning. When you feel compassion for someone else (without pitying them) you understand that suffering, mistakes, and imperfection are shared human qualities. You feel warmth, affection, and a desire to help the person towards whom your compassion is directed. People feel compassion because they understand that every human being deserves support and understanding, regardless of whether they have some special set of characteristics (such as beauty, intelligence, certain talents, and so on).

Yet many find it difficult to show compassion toward themselves and may even feel uncomfortable when compassion is directed at them. Feeling friendly toward yourself, being warm and kind to yourself, and embracing yourself with affection and love can be so alien that you may need a long time to develop these abilities. A person who struggles to be compassionate towards him- or herself may at the same time find it easy to show others compassion.

Just as you are understanding and compassionate towards others over their mistakes and behavior, you can show yourself compassion when you go through difficulties, make mistakes, or become aware of something you dislike about yourself. Rather than pushing difficult feelings away, you pause and say to yourself: "Ah, this is so difficult right now. How can I be compassionate and sensitive towards myself at this moment?"

Compassion is also about acknowledging that you are imperfect and have many flaws. All human beings do. But you deserve compassion, like everyone else. Accept yourself the way you are. Who says you have to be perfect and able to handle everything? By showing yourself compassion, you honor and recognize everything that is entailed in being human. You won't get everything you want in this life, nor will you want everything you get. You will go through difficulties. You will face loss in some form or other. You will make mistakes. You will be forced to own up to your own limitations. This is the human condition, a reality that we all share as human beings. The more willing you are to open your eyes and accept this reality instead of fighting it, the better you will be prepared to be compassionate toward yourself.

SELF-PITY AND SELF-INDULGENCE

When you pity yourself, you become consumed with your own problems and forget that others may have similar difficulties. People in the throes of self-pity reject shared human experience, distance themselves from others, and feel that they alone suffer. Self-pity can make people egocentric, causing them to ascribe too much importance to their own suffering. Self-compassion, on the other hand, enables us to see our own suffering in the context of others' pain without the need to isolate ourselves from others. A person who pities himself becomes consumed with his own emotional problems and cannot see beyond them. He cannot take a step back and evaluate the situation deliberately and neutrally. But by looking at a situation with compassion for ourselves, we can give ourselves emotional "breathing space" that enables us to recognize that our personal suffering is not so different from the suffering of others.

Being compassionate toward yourself does not imply self-indulgence. Some people are reluctant to show themselves compassion because they fear that if they do, they will allow themselves to get away with almost everything. "I'm feeling stressed out today, and so I'm going to be nice to myself and just watch TV and eat lots of ice cream." This line of thinking is a case of indulgence or escapism rather than compassion. Constant self-indulgence distances us from our own emotions. Compassion, on the other hand, helps us to take small steps in the direction of better health and more happiness.

THREE ELEMENTS OF COMPASSION

KINDNESS AND WARMTH

Self-compassion entails that we be warm and kind toward ourselves, especially in difficult times. People who are compassionate toward themselves know that imperfection, difficulty, and mistakes are inevitable. They have developed the habit of treating themselves with consideration and kindness when they face suffering and difficulty, rather than responding in anger and blaming others for their misfortune when life doesn't meet their expectations.

COMMON HUMAN EXPERIENCE

When things don't go our way and we feel disappointed and powerless, irrational and overwhelming emotions may seize hold of us. We feel that I must be the only person in the world who suffers or makes mistakes. But everyone suffers sometimes. The very definition of being "human" necessitates that we be mortal, vulnerable, and imperfect. Self-compassion entails a realization that suffering and a feeling of inadequacy is a common thread in all human experience. Compassion requires us to realize that we all go through these feelings, rather than thinking that I am the only person who suffers and everyone else must be happier than me.

In this context, we must be aware that factors like family history, culture, genetics, and the environment all affect our thoughts, emotions, and behaviors. It is worth reminding ourselves that there are many circumstances in our lives that we haven't chosen, and that a great deal of what happens to us is not our own fault. Some result from a variety of factors, including genetics and environment, and we have little or no control. If people had full control over their behavior, how many would make a conscious choice in favor of anger, addiction, social phobia, anxiety, or an eating disorder? If we realize that we share a common reality as human beings and are both dependent on each other and in many ways alike, we don't have to take things quite so personally. Be compassionate and understanding towards yourself and recognize that mistakes and struggles are a part of life – not just your life, but everyone's life.

MINDFULNESS

Mindfulness is about living in the moment – paying attention to what happens here and now without weighing and measuring everything constantly. Mindfulness is devoting your attention to the moment, independent of extraneous thought, existing in the present. It is often good to begin the practice of mindfulness by withdrawing a little from the chaos of daily life. When you become accustomed to that, you can practice mindfulness under any circumstances. When you eat, for instance, you keep your attention on the task at hand. When you read a book, you don't do anything but read. When you play with a child, you devote your undivided attention to the game.

With mindfulness, you can observe thoughts as they come and go without becoming absorbed in what you are thinking. Thoughts have a tendency to wander and can gather in the mind from all directions. By practicing mindfulness, you reduce the distracting effect of wandering thoughts. While you are mindful, thoughts do not penetrate as deeply into your mind, though they return quickly when you drop the mindfulness.

By being aware in this way you can observe when a thought enters your mind and when it leaves. Instead of allowing a thought to take over your mind, you allow it to pass by like a cloud in a blue sky. Paying attention to it is in truth an act of witnessing something. You bear witness to your thinking, bear witness to your breathing. You pay attention to everything without judging it, without evaluating it, because as soon as you do that, you are inviting the thoughts in. When you are in a mindful state, you occupy a neutral space. The strongest way of being mindful and in the now is to concentrate on your breathing and observe it.

ANNA'S STORY

A CHALLENGE

In this book I tell my personal story of bereavement when my husband, Árni, was diagnosed with cancer in November 1996 and died seven months later. We have three daughters who were four, six and twelve years old at the time. I started my story when he became ill, and then I had no intention for it to appear to the public. But as time passed I felt that my writings might be helpful to other people, both those who are in mourning and others who want to look into the world of grief. As I wrote down these fragments of my life at this difficult time, I found a close confidant on the blank page or on the white screen of my computer, and I used both. In my story, I describe in detail how I experienced my husband's illness and his death. I talk about the process of my grief and how I survived this painful experience that sometimes I thought had no end to it. I also mention how parenthood took a lot of my strength and how the role of the one living parent expands when the other is not present anymore.

Reading books helped me and influenced my attitude, two books in particular, by authors who have been tested greatly, as laymen and professionals, who have suffered themselves and dealt with the pain of others. These books fascinated me and I wanted to connect with the authors; and this did happen. The books are *Man's Search for Meaning* by Viktor E. Frankl and The Wheel of Life, the autobiography of Elisabeth Kübler-Ross.

Viktor E. Frankl (1905-1997) was an Austrian psychiatrist and psychoanalyst. He wrote his story, *Man's Search for Meaning*, after surviving in Auschwitz. Frankl describes human suffering and humiliation at its worst. I found it unbelievable how he was able to raise his mind and awareness above the pain and helplessness while he could at the same time use the witness's eye that led him into a deeper understanding of human nature and behavior. He writes that each one of us can find his or her own personal meaning of life and that it is important for us to do so. If we cannot find a meaning to life, Frankl suggests we should seek to awaken our willingness within, in order to find our own special meaning. He says that people are able to find the meaning in three ways: by working on a particular project, through love or through suffering. Frankl's book had a great influence on me. It was published in Icelandic translation at the time when my husband was dying. I was impressed by Frankl's honest and forthright narrative. I bought several copies and gave them to friends, doctors and hospitals.

I had a longing to meet Frankl, go abroad and visit him, this now-aged man, and thank him and tell him how significant his story had been for me during the most difficult time of my life. I spoke about this to a friend who was a great admirer of Frankl's and he told me that the man had a web page. I checked it out and found two telephone numbers listed there. Before I knew it, I had picked up the phone and dialed one of the numbers. I waited with bated breath, while it rang on the other end of the line. Then I heard a voice; this was the voice of Viktor Frankl himself, who said, "Hello."

My heart was pounding in my chest while I tried to explain the reason for my phone call. We spoke in English. I told him that I lived in Iceland and that I had recently read his book.

"Oh, has it been translated in Icelandic now?" he said. I told him about the illness and death of my husband and how powerful I felt his story was and how it had helped me in my suffering. He commiserated with me and said he was glad that his book had been useful and helpful to me.

"It's good for me to hear that, then it's easier for me to die," said Viktor Frankl, and that was the end of our conversation. Frankl died a few weeks later at the age of ninety-two.

The second book, *The Wheel of Life*, I read one or two years after Árni died. The author, Elisabeth Kübler-Ross (1926-2004), was born in Switzerland and worked for decades as a psychiatrist in the USA. I had earlier read her book *On Death and Dyin*g, in which she describes how as a resident physician she began working in a ward for terminally ill patients where no one, neither staff, nor relatives nor patients dared to mention death. Ross approached the patients directly and it turned out that most of them, if not all, were aware of their dying. Despite this fact the doctors acted as if things were going fine and they didn't even inform their patients of their incurable disease. Death was never mentioned. Ross dared to approach the subject of death. I became absolutely fascinated by her honesty and acquired her autobiography, *The Wheel of Life*, which is the life story of a woman who, in a remarkable way, showed both professionalism and deep intuition while working with people who were mentally or physically ill, and taught them how to deal with death. She was a psychiatrist like Frankl. I also felt a desire to meet her. In her story she says that she is a lover of chocolate, and I thought how enjoyable it would be if I could visit her and bring her dark chocolate from Iceland.

In her book she said that she lived in Phoenix, Arizona, USA. I had recently finished a yoga teacher training at Kripalu Center and Kevin, one of my fellow students from the training, lived in Arizona. I decided to ask him about Ross, whether he knew anything about her. But I didn't do it at once; some weeks or months passed. Then one morning, without reflection, I sat down and wrote him an email where I told him about her and how amazing I thought her book was and that I would very much like to meet her and give her some chocolate! I asked him if he knew anything about her, if she was still working, if he could inquire about her, and if she was still in good health.

Early next morning, Kevin had replied to my email. "Anna, this is incredible!" He'd read my email in the morning, just before he went to a conference for physiotherapists. And he continued: "Guess who one of the lecturers was? Elisabeth Kübler-Ross! I was thrilled and after her lecture I went to see her and told her about you. She was in a wheelchair but otherwise in good health. She asked me to give you her greetings and tell you that she is still keeping busy!"

I was astonished to read Kevin's message. Two weeks later Kevin had a stroke and never recovered fully after that.

I have many times thought of the meaning of these connections with Frankl and Ross, who both have influenced millions of people all around the world. I have chosen to use these connections as a challenge to share the experience of my husband's death with others, in an open and honest way.

TO ANNA

When bends and breaks my living wave
Yours will arise again
And strong you stand in the life you gave
Your warmths for me remain.

When and how our paths may lie
To that I have no answer
But follow you awhile I may
With love for you, my dancer.

(Árni)

MY BELOVED

I know that my beloved would want me to make every effort to be happy, to be grateful for the time that we had together. My beloved would want me to make an effort to work with my emotions so that I could better support our children, all of whom I love, and others in their mourning. My beloved would want me to allow myself to be sensitive, to cry, to feel pain, to miss. My beloved would want me to say his name with a smile on my lips. My beloved would want me to say that life is too big for me to understand it all but I would try to endure what life hands to me. My beloved would want me to know that he did not wish to depart from here and leave me, but it was not up to him to make that decision. Life itself brought both of us this task; I did not wish for it and he did not wish for it. You cannot always get what you wish for and you do not wish for everything you get. My beloved would whisper to me, "Look at this as an opportunity, and look at my death as a chance for you to deepen yourself, to appreciate life more, to become a better person, to make a change, to let your dreams come true." My beloved would say, "Cry, but be happy."

OUR STORY

Árni and I met through the Junior Chamber organization. I lived in Gardabær, an urban community near Reykjavík, while he lived in Keflavik, a neighboring community. I had been a member for two years and got to know some very good people through my involvement. I learned how to run meetings, organize committee work and public speaking events. Árni and I met at meetings and gatherings and soon began to notice each other. He was four years older than I. We started dating and fell in love. After a few months I became pregnant and we started living together, in Keflavik where we found an apartment on the ground floor. Árni owned a small printing business during this period but it was hard to keep it running. Our oldest daughter was born in the fall and within that next year we moved to a village in East Iceland, Egilsstadir. The operation of the print shop ended with bankruptcy.

When we moved to Egilsstadir, Árni started working in another print shop, while I got a job selling furniture. We had little means and lived sparingly, but we were able to pay up our debts by keeping our budget tight, being careful not to overspend on anything, and I sewed all the clothing for the family. We worked well together, rationed our disposable funds in the same manner as the saving experts teach people to do today. It worked well for us. We participated in the social life of Egilsstadir, continued working with the JC, and we took an active part in various local unions through the years. This was a fruitful time; we made some good friends and we felt that life was good in our village. When our oldest daughter was six years old, another girl was born to us and our third daughter came about two years later. Life was good, there was more than enough to do, and it was good to raise children in a small community. We enjoyed life.

We sometimes traveled to Reykjavík to meet the family at large. Every once in a while we were able to go somewhere, just the two of us, and we would have liked to have the chance to do so more often.

Árni was great a dad and a good mentor to our daughters. He was a quiet man and shy by nature. Still, he was sociable, having participated, as a young man, in an amateur acting club. He was the chairman of the sports association Hottur in Egilsstadir for several years. He had good qualities and spoke well of others. In meetings he often asked to speak after the rest had loudly revealed their opinion, and when he spoke he got everyone's attention. He seemed to give himself ample time to consider his thoughts and ideas before he voiced them. Árni was humorous and had an even temper. He often smiled and laughed when I saw the more serious side of the matter. He was artistic and was at his best when he was expressing his creativity. He drew and painted artwork in his leisure time. On his deathbed, he told me how upset and distressed he had been after he and his childhood friend, whom he had established the print shop with, had ended their lifelong friendship. The difficulties in running the operation, misunderstanding and unfinished business resulted in his friend leaving the business and they never spoke again.

Árni was true a mediator. "Some truths are to be left unspoken," he often said if my temper got the best of me. I was more of a butterfly than he was and sometimes needed little to upset me. We were good at discussing matters and we agreed on how to raise our daughters. We held hands up the steep paths and down to the hollows, but we also had good periods that we savored. We enjoyed being together and we were able to work harmoniously on creative tasks. We established an advertising agency, Árni´s dream project, and worked together on many ideas, some turning out successful. Árni was able to use his creative abilities to the full and received several awards for logo proposals that he sent in to competitions. After having lived twelve years in Egilsstadir, Árni died, and three years later I moved to Gardabaer in the capital area with our daughters.

I REMEMBER this moment so clearly. As if it had been only yesterday. I stood by the sink, washing the dishes, the plates and glasses that I'd washed a hundred, maybe a thousand times before. I wasn't thinking of anything in specific, not even about the plates washed over and over again. Not pondering how often they'd been washed, would be washed, where they came from or where they would end. I'd never given it a thought and it didn't enter my mind now where I stood, a woman in a kitchen, washing the dishes. I was home alone with two of our daughters, expecting our third child, though I didn't show yet. Only I and my husband knew. I sometimes wondered if it was too big a task to handle, to become a mother of three. We'd wanted to have one more child, yet I was alarmed when I discovered that I was pregnant. I knew that it wasn't only about longing for a child, or just to carry a baby. To have a baby was much more than that. And I sensed some risk in being pregnant. But I was also aware that all human relations, all projects entail a risk. Life itself is a risk. I'd often thought about it.

But right at this moment, doing the dishes, I wasn't thinking of anything in particular. Not even this. I stood there and completed the task for the task itself. This is how women do the dishes. It's how they attend to their home, fold the laundry. This is how they prepare a future for their children. I was sometimes submerged in thoughts at the sink. In fact, I'd gotten remarkably many good ideas doing these chores, these routine tasks that couldn't wait, that held life in a fixed place, and provided safety for my children. I looked empty-minded down into the soap, did circles with the brush. Endless circles of cleanliness, lathering up, then down. It foamed quite nicely, this advertised washing-up liquid. Maybe I was in a sort of a trance. Where is the mind when it's not thinking? Is it nowhere? Is it on vacation? Is it aware of itself? But no, I wasn't thinking at all. Not about my mind either. Watched and worked. Stood there, a woman expecting, did the dishes after dinner. Looked out of the window, saw half of the night and herself reflected in the window.

Suddenly, I saw a face. The face of my father-in-law. It appeared for one split second and then it was gone. It conveyed a silent message. I knew what the message was. Sensed it.

It entered me instantaneously. Changed me. Could my mind have been out there getting this message? It entered me in a flash and rushed down my body. Prevented my hands from going in circles. Clean circles. All became still. I looked at my reflection in the window glass with the night in the background. The dark background. Night. Darkness. Why wasn't it day time? Why was this taking place? Where did it come from? I shook my head and at the same time tried to rid my body of the numbness. Involuntarily, my left hand started to move in circles. I narrowed my eyes, peering out into the dark, seeing nothing but black and my own reflection. There was nothing there. This was nothing. Just some nonsense I'd made up myself.

My mind ran in circles. How could this happen? I stood there as I had been standing every day for weeks, months, years, doing the dishes. An ordinary woman attending to the daily household chores. What was different now? In some eerie moment, the face of my father-in-law had appeared before me in the dark. We were good companions, he and I, but not close friends. We had mutual respect for each other. Then he came to me now and showed me his face. A face without the glance of the eye: mute. Yet it conveyed to me a message that I felt inside.

A message that my husband would die.

My husband. Die. Who could send such a message? Who could know such a thing? Of course, we would all die in the end. That much is certain.

My mind was mesmerized. I made every effort to erase this encounter. Downplay it. Said to myself in my mind that it was some nonsense. There was nothing logical about this experience. But I was ambivalent about it. Why had this appeared in front of me? Could this be right? Could I be making this up myself? Was this maybe what I wished, without realizing it? Suddenly, all the dishes were done. Nothing was left in the sink.

I took the washcloth and soaked it in the water as I always did. The cloth was clean. I loved the smell of clean rags. Clean cloths make dirty surfaces spotless. I was no rag type, though. In fact, I found housecleaning tedious. But was ok with doing the dishes. Probably because of the many good ideas being born there.

I wrung the cloth from the hot water. Breathed in the clean smell of the cloth. Went to the table and wiped off food crumbs and water drops. Erased the recent dinner. With a clean rag. This couldn't have happened. I hadn't received this message. My husband was not about to die. It was not I who was standing here, wiping the table, overwhelmed by this instant message out of the dark. I was determined not to let this rule my emotions. But nevertheless, the fear remained in there. Defenseless, I had received it. Was it to take roots in me? I was expecting a baby. I pictured my baby in my womb. Above the baby I had consented to foster the fear. It was there. I felt it clearly. I suddenly felt sick.

From then on I was almost constantly fearful about my husband. I was always afraid that he would die and I'd lose him. I could feel the child growing in my womb and I feared that my husband would never get to see it. Kept calling him on the phone. If he went on a shorter or longer business trip I demanded that he would constantly keep me notified where he was. I warned him about slippery roads and speeding. Told him I was feeling uneasy. But never told him what I was really feeling. How could I? He closely observed my womb getting larger. We often watched how my womb quivered when the baby moved. But he never was allowed to gain knowledge about the other fetus. The one that made me sad inside. The one that held me in the clutches of eerie insecurity and constant fear. I feared that I would find him dead in our bed when I woke in the morning. I feared to receive a phone call that something horrible had happened to him. I couldn't let go of this feeling. I lived with it, unable to share it with anyone, carried it alone. And after I gave birth to our youngest daughter the fear was still there. As time passed, and all the work took over–child raising, running our business with all that it entailed–the fear diminished and gradually, softly, and quietly disappeared.

When our youngest daughter was one year old my father-in-law got ill and medical examination revealed that he had prostate cancer. He went through several treatments and struggled for his life and fought the disease for one year until, overcome by this illness, he died. This made me certain that I had misunderstood the message. Of course I had. The message was obvious now. My father-in-law had appeared to me and told me of a death. Not the death of his son, but his own death. There was no doubt about it. I had clearly misunderstood the message.

Again, child care and the daily routine took over. There were always plenty of things that needed to be done. It was important to tend well to the business so our home would receive enough financial means. During this period I took part in establishing a hand-craft business along with several other women. This was modern life. Loads of work. Brimming with plans. Lacking time. Full of duties. Little time for leisure. Lot of work. Less of free time. And the clock ticked. The clock of life. Weeks. Months. Years.

For some time Árni had been losing weight and feeling pain in his stomach. We were having lunch during our lunch break.

I opened the fridge. It was full of food.

I called to him, "Árni, aren't you going to eat the meat dish from yesterday?"

"No, thanks, I don't want any, could you maybe make a light soup?"

“What about the fish from the day before yesterday? It’ll start to spoil. Should I reheat it for you?”

Árni always took care of leftovers. He was a hearty eater, living with four women who ate more from necessity than for pleasure. I scanned the food supplies in the fridge thoroughly. When we were in a hurry at lunch time, I often saw only what was at the front in the fridge. I scanned further this time. The fridge was full of leftovers. Árni had not been doing his share in finishing them as he normally did.

”No, Anna, I just feel like having a bowl of soup right now.”

At this point, right at this very moment, I felt a throbbing bad feeling inside. Something wasn’t as it should be. If my Árni wasn’t able to eat, something was definitely wrong. This something was not a good sign. I stood up, closed the fridge and slowly walked into the living room. He was lying on the sofa. That also told me something was wrong. I looked at him closely. He had lost weight. His appetite had not been good recently. I looked at him more closely. He normally didn’t lie down during lunchtime.

“Árni, are you feeling unwell?”

“I’m not feeling too good in my stomach.”

“You know, now that I am looking at you, I can see that you’ve lost some of weight.”

“Yes, I’ve lost over twenty pounds.”

“Over twenty pounds! Is that true?”

Suddenly, I saw it clearly.

What was happening? How could I have missed this? Was I fast asleep? My husband had lost twenty pounds and I’d hardly noticed. Where were my eyes? Where was my awareness? Why didn’t I see this earlier? I could’ve done something.

“My dear Árni, you normally eat all the leftovers from the fridge. Have you spoken with a doctor?”

“No, but I’m going to call him later today. Just give me some soup now.”

Our lunch was very light this particular day. But a heavy feeling in the chest. To my knowledge, Árni had just once before seen a doctor, when he’d caught a bad flu. He had been healthy all his life. Apart from that he had trouble with his digestive system from time to time. A doctor years ago had said that his colon was extra-long. That doctor had examined him when he was a young boy because of constant problems with the digestion. Árni had learned to live with that fact and it caused him discomfort only once in a while.

Odd, how the most peculiar things can take place right in front of your eyes and you take no notice, until suddenly. Then, it’s as if something has already happened. Like it isn’t taking place any longer in the now. But something that has already occurred and now belongs to the past. And you start blaming yourself for not having seen it. For having been blind. For having done nothing. But feeling that you could have done something. Árni went to the doctor. He had edema on his legs. Further examination revealed that his metabolism wasn’t functioning as it should. He suffered from excessive swelling in the digestive canal and got a prescription for strong a vitamin and steroid treatment in order to decrease it. I feared that this might be some malignant disease but the examination gave no indication of that. He was diagnosed with gluten intolerance.

He came home after a two-week stay in hospital. Caught one illness after another and had to stay home from work for several weeks. Then he started to get better. But he needed to remain on a special diet and was not allowed to eat cereals, wheat and the most common kinds of flour. After a few months he got worse and was examined again.

Another steroid treatment followed, and better health. Then about a year after the first diagnosis, he became seriously ill and was operated on. Then it was all revealed.

I walked slowly into the Intensive Care at the Akureyri Hospital after his first operation. He lay there, his body connected to all kinds of tubes. I could see that he felt better.

"Hello, darling."

I walked to him, kissed him. We were somehow torn and twisted on the inside with anguish, baffled with confusion over the circumstances that we suddenly found ourselves in. Our friend was with me. He had driven me nearly 200 miles from Egilsstadir to Akureyri, northern Iceland, the same route as Árni had gone in an ambulance two days earlier.

"You're feeling much better now, I can see that," I said. I could still see he was in pain, though, sleepy and numb. He had trouble speaking and less endurance. Everything about him was white and somehow cold but also at the same time warm somehow; he clearly felt warm in his bed.

The doctor entered.

"How do you do, I not meet you before," he said with a foreign accent.

"How do you do, no we haven't met but we've spoken on the phone," I said.

He shook my hand cheerfully. It was a firm handshake. On almost every finger he wore silver rings, reminding me of a philanderer from some exotic country. Árni had told me about the rings. He was tall, standing with his feet splayed out, wearing jeans and a plaid shirt. Tinted skin. An Italian, raised in New York. Long and curly hair, and a rather long, full beard. His hair just starting to turn grey at his temples. A handsome man. We sat down, on either side of the bed.

"I want to say you immediately, that this disease is serious. I learn that it is best to be honest with my patients. Better tell truth."

He described the disease, explaining in detail where it was located in the digestive canal and that this was with the first incidence of this kind of cancer in Iceland. Only a handful of cases like this were known around the world. At a large hospital in Iowa in the US, doctors knew of six such cases. He pointed out the importance of fighting and never losing hope.

"There is great hope in fighting," he said.

"We do all we can."

He then repeated all he had said about the disease itself, the hope, and how serious the situation was. We had to ask questions more than once and sometimes more than twice. It wasn't always easy to understand him. But he gave us ample time.

"We speak with Sweden and USA," he said.

"They say chemotherapy is best option. Sweden say six treatments, USA say eight, we do eight times."

I got a convulsive feeling in my stomach. Everything went black. I felt dizzy.

"You get five types of medications. Very toxic. Difficult treatment. No other options. We must fight. You begin chemotherapy tomorrow."

He watched us with his brown eyes that came from elsewhere than this cold icy country where he now said these chilly words. We were all silent. Despair and hope fought against each other in my mind. My antipathy to drugs increased.

"Isn't there any medication from plants available? Some herbal medicine? I know a woman who takes such medication. Can't we ... is this the only way?"

I couldn't bear to think of you taking these toxic doses that could maybe finish you. Why had this to be so? Where was science? Where was respect for life? Did this mean that life was respected? What about emotions? Why was it acceptable to administer medicine for a human that had power and toxicity similar to that of a nuclear weapon and did not only attack the target but everything else around it? If we think of the planet as one body, it would be illegal to use such weapons. Weapons that shoot down innocent individuals, break down their houses and destroy all that has been built up. War. Air raid imminent. I became stuffed with anxiety. Something cracked inside me. No, this can't be! These drugs are so strong that they kill people. I can't go along with this.

I cried. I felt acutely my total helplessness in this whole situation. First, it was not my body, and second, I had no professional knowledge in this matter. I just had an inner feeling that such medicine was poisonous. This was my unwavering position towards it. It was his body, but it was our life. I had neither voting rights nor even the right to make proposals. Using them was the only solution after a thorough medical evaluation. The only correct way for hope. The disease was serious. What did that mean? Was it the route to the end of life? Were there other sides to the matter? Was it only medical? Despite a comfortable bed, a warm duvet, intravenous nutrition, pain medication, bathing, encouragement, ambitious nursing, we had now lost our independence. You didn't have any jurisdiction over your body. It was in the hands of other people now. Some people elsewhere in the world decided what was best for you. I wasn't counted in. I didn't own you. I thought of herbal medication. I had to try to do something.

"I've heard about a German doctor who lives in the United States. He has developed medicine against cancer. This medicine is illegal here but he sells it widely in many countries in the world. I would like to check on this."

"You do that. There are various kinds of medicine available. Most don't work. But we start chemotherapy," the doctor said. "These drugs give hope of good prognosis."

He watched me with a look in his eyes of the one who knows better from experience. He pretended that he believed what I said but he didn't really. I realized that if a patient wants to take herbal medication and have naturopathy for his disease, he must fight for it himself. Rise, dead sick from the warm bed of the hospital, and travel across continents, all at his own cost. Take responsibility for his own health, own life. Sacrifice everything for his health. Take the risk. I had neither the option nor the authority to tamper with Árni's medical treatment. I had no say in the matter. He lay there in the warm bed, unable to stand up yet. He looked out of the window, in the direction of the cemetery.

"I want to fight. I want to go through with this. I have complete faith in you," he said to the doctor.

You were given information sheets about the effects of the medication and their side effects, which to me were horrible. I was defensive. I experienced the threat of the disease, but I felt that the threat of the medication was even more ominous. But you were optimistic; there was joy and hope in your voice when you said, "The evil must be run out with another evil." You smiled. I thought much about your words. They were not in your usual spirit. You didn't live that kind of life. If someone wronged you, you never stood up with a vengeful mind. You retreated in peace with the conviction that the other person didn't realize what he was doing. You allowed time to settle the case. Then, you entered with your strength when the anger had abated in the other person. And then the grounds had changed. I thought, how can this chemo work for him?

In my heart I didn't believe that it would win. To my eyes, the therapy was the revenge. The revenge that gets back at the enemy, that destroys and damages. But medically this was our only hope. I also understood that the hope is found within the medical system and in the methods practiced in clinical medicine. There, chemotherapy is not seen as revenge or a weapon of mass destruction, but as a hope for cure. I had so often been critical and prejudiced toward the public health care system and its methodology. Yet, the hospital welcomes the patients with singular care. There he gets a bed and all the nursing and care that he needs. The hospital welcomes him with arms wide open and brings him in from the cold and into the warmth. In from the fear, in to the hope. In from isolation, in to a community. Surrounded by wonderful people, individuals who have chosen as their path in life to care for the sick. For the weak. For those with failing strength, some of whom face death.

It was spring time. You were at the Akureyri Hospital. I stayed overnight with some friends who lived in the town. They always made hot chocolate on weekends. They were good and warm people. It was hot chocolate day today. Saturday. It was cozy to drink it first thing in the morning. This was a wonderful spring morning in every way except for that you were ill and we weren't together. The family wasn't together. Our oldest daughter was in Egilsstadir. She stayed with her friend's family and was playing football with her team. She played for you. She did well. For you. Our two younger ones were in Reykjavík. Their granny and aunt took turns looking after them. Mostly their granny. They had each other. Supported each other. Comforted each other in their fear. They were so young, only four and six. Still, they realized that something bad was happening. You were ill. So very ill. For such a long time. I told them that our life was about to change.

"Mommy, our life is about to change," our youngest daughter repeated.

"Yes, my love, our life is about to change," I confirmed.

That was it. Our life had already changed, taken on a different hue. Everything was different. Our daily thoughts were different and our daily emotions were not the same as before. There was now some deep undertone that resounded with a heavy rhythm. It wasn't audible all the time but it seemed always to be there, somewhere in the back. Beyond what was seen. Beneath what took place on the surface.

The hot chocolate was tasty. It felt so nice to be able to sit down and drink a cup that someone had made for me. The spring was dancing outside. Life-giving spring, reviving spring. You didn't get to enjoy any of the gifts of this spring. You lay in a white bed, in a white room, in a white hospital. You were white yourself. I finished my cup and the refreshments. My day was beginning. I was on my way to you. Into your white world. I was always impatient to get to you. I never wanted to be late. Stayed with you the whole day. Sometimes, I went away just for short time, went swimming or to make a call. But I didn't want to be away too long. Thought something might happen to you while I was away and wasn't taking care of you.

I thanked my friends for the hot chocolate and left for the hospital. As I was in the driveway on my way to the car I saw them. The couple in the house across the street. They were working in their garden. A little girl was running around them playfully. They turned their back to me and didn't see me. Didn't know that I was sneaking into their world. I watched this family with envious eyes as they were doing spring chores, which I've never found enjoyable myself. Watched the little girl, playing safely in the company of her parents. This sight revealed to me a life that I had had before but didn't have anymore. I had begun to miss you. I had lost a part of you. I had lost you from our spring chores in our garden. You wouldn't mow the lawn this summer. I would be the one to do that. It was all right. I was fully capable of mowing the grass. I opened the door and sat in the car. Dried the tears from my cheeks and backed out of the driveway. Started driving, on my way to you.

AFTER THE first operation on Árni, I had a sense of foreboding. An uneasy feeling that this disease would continue to invade his body and there was only a question when it would recur. He had been diagnosed with tumors in the small intestines. The consequences were perforated intestines due to the tumors, so that the content of the intestines leaked out into the abdominal cavity, which in turn caused internal infection and he became seriously ill. I had the feeling that there was a ticking time bomb in his stomach. I was preoccupied with this thought at first. But he did respond well to the chemo, which we had been warned could be very difficult. He received the medication through intravenous infusion, and that took 24-48 hours. He withstood it all. Yet, we'd been told that he would definitely be confined to bed for certain periods during the administration of the medicine. He seemed not to pay much attention to this information, or to follow its prediction. He was in good spirits and said he was doing fine. He was always cold, though, and wore woolen underwear both in cold and warm weather. He immersed himself in work and only wanted to spend his time at his workplace.

I worried about him. Thought he should relax and rest. But I had no say in how he chose to work, no more today than any other day. Work meant much to him. He felt so good being out in the field again. To be at the wheel in his own company. A business that he had built up with hope, optimism and his own hard work. Now he was again in direct contact with life itself. He had a good assistant who had been recruited just two weeks before Árni fell ill. But I would rather that Árni stayed at home, drinking hot herbal tea and eating my special home-baked bread. That he would be in my special care. So that I could keep an eye on him and be ready if something came up. He was keen on swimming. Didn't mind the lack of hair at all. Still, it was a change for people to see him with a fair complexion. He, who'd had dark brown hair and always worn a beard.

A young boy once asked him at a sports game, "Why don't you have any hair on your head?"

"Don't you think this looks cool?" Árni asked him and ran his hand over his bald head.

"I think it looks good. It looks like Michael Jordan. You know he hasn't got any hair on his head."

Árni was often tired and at times he suffered from pain in his stomach. Everything was tinged by his illness. There were no visions or plans for the future. We tried as hard as we could to keep our usual pace and it took all our effort. We decided not to build the new house that we'd been planning for some years. We'd bought a building site and a blueprint. Our plan had been to build a wooden house with two floors and paint it red with white window frames and a black roof. He said that the future was unclear for everyone. Because no one really knew what would happen the next day.

I think that his view of the vague future enabled him in some way to live for each moment and experience the present more acutely. At least I often thought he radiated some inner beauty that I had never seen in him before. It was as if the illness forced his back against the wall and woke something within him. As if his attitude had changed. Until work consumed him completely. He'd had a tendency to overexert himself in his work; he'd sometimes work from dawn till dusk, with little enthusiasm on my part. I felt that work was stealing him away from me. But he was so happy being able to work again. That meant he was out in life. Out in his business. Steering his own ship.

The extremes tips you off the fine line of balance. When this happens, some aspects of life become overfed while others are undernourished. I felt this was the case with us. But in between were periods when we found our balance and life was more agreeable. The months during the chemotherapy were tough. A heavy undertow incessantly pulled our boat of life. Every month, Árni was to receive the poison, the strong concoction that may or may not knock him out.

We felt anxiety, restlessness and irritation when the injection periods drew nearer. There was something dreadful about this. And the outcome was uncertain. After the ultrasound graphics were done, when he had finished one or two chemo doses, there was indication of a better prognosis. This gave us hope. The medicine was working. Was successful. It was worth taking. The wheels were turning. We strove for keeping them in the tracks.

But after five sessions of the chemo he got weaker. He had to work less. Spend more time in my embrace. He still gritted his teeth and bore with it, and continued working. He also drank my herbal tea more often. The sixth chemo was postponed for two weeks. He wasn't feeling good enough. Then a short while later he was given the sixth dose. Felt weak and frequently needed to lie down for a nap. Shivered on the sofa under the blanket. He got severe side effects. Pain in the groin. Felt pain during urination and there was blood in his urine: known side effects. Less appetite and sometimes pain in his abdomen, too.

ONE NIGHT, we were at a local gathering. It was an accordion music contest. We sat there dressed up having dinner with 200 other people. It was your chemo period and your bald head shone from every angle in the hall. I remember how preoccupied I was with your hair loss. I loved your beard. Only once in our relationship did you shave it off. I thought you looked more stunningly handsome with your hair and your beard but when you lost both I thought you were just as good-looking. You handled this with style. You were so beautiful and radiant and you stood up for yourself. No regrets, no tears. Were you feeling happiness for being given one more day here on earth? I didn't know your thoughts entirely but I grasped that you recognized that your life was getting shorter. This was both plain and tacit in the poems you wrote.

So, we sat there at the accordion contest. I've never particularly enjoyed that kind of music. I prefer free-style music, music that you can dance freely to. You had more sense of rhythm on the dance floor and were an excellent dancer. Gliding effortlessly over the dance floor with the various women at the yearly Thor's feast, the midwinter festival, while your wife danced free-style with various men. We also danced together. Sometimes I danced your ballroom way. Most often, I got into trouble, taking a step out of rhythm with you, so my toes would sometimes land under or on yours. But that never stopped us from dancing together in your style, and we just thought it was amusing.

The celebration was starting. The program was introduced and a young man came on stage singing an old pop song before the contest started. The song was called "I Live In a Dream." It was one of my old favorites and I knew the lyrics. The young man performed perfectly and the accordion festival began.

Two weeks later we were on our way home from work to eat lunch at home. We stopped by the grocery store and I was about to step out of the car when we saw the singer coming out of the store, holding his shopping bag.

Then you suddenly said, "

I would like to have that song at my funeral, the one that he sang at the accordion competition."

I was a bit startled. Didn't find the right words in response. I understood you, though, because I found the song appealing.

"Oh, you would?"

I opened the car door and stepped out. Breathed in the cooling air. He knew! He had the courage to express it. He gave me a message. He looked down the road; this was his route. He was preparing us for what would come to pass. Wanted to have a say in the matter. "I live in a dream, I don't draw the line between the day and the night, I just swing involuntarily," the lyrics said. Did he experience his life as a pendulum in the life clock, with only a few tics left? I felt the fresh air on my body as I spun lightly down the steps to the small grocery store.

❀

WITHIN WEEKS, he was back at Akureyri Hospital. The bomb within had exploded. He was more ill than ever. I went home for two days to do a few things. Pay the bills for the business and our household. I would have liked not to have to do these errands but taking care of those ordinary tasks, no matter what else was going on, kept me grounded and connected to daily life. There were all sort of things I had to do on my own. Nothing gets done on its own and nothing can be taken for granted. No one appears out of the blue and takes the responsibility of your life for you. Everyone has their limits. People give of themselves what they can according to their own nature. And of course, there's no one who can take on the task of paying someone else's bills. Financial matters are private, just like sex. However, people showed their support by opening an account for our family and depositing money into it. Having discussed between themselves the horrible situation that we found ourselves in, a number of people wished to contribute. Wished to come to our aid. Realized that in all this incredible helplessness, one way to support us was to raise money. Relieve us of some of our burden, at least in this one way.

There was still the enormous effort to face the loss of health that reduces the ability to nurse your own life. The capability to build your own future. People were generous, kind-hearted and showed sympathy. Maybe they looked into their own circumstances and felt thankful that it wasn't them who had to face bad health. Maybe they got a lump in the throat when they saw us in the super market. Maybe they were filled with silent despair, sensed the world's helplessness and unfairness when they saw our daughters. Watching them, children among other children. They weren't in any way different from the rest of the children in the group. Except in the mind of those who knew what was happening. Knew whose children they were and what the real situation was at home.

Still, the reality in children's lives can have many facets. It could be that the reality of our children was no worse than that of many other children, even if it seemed to be. Things are not always as they appear to be. Those particular children had never experienced aggressive behavior or violence from their father. Only tenderness and affection no matter what. He did spend a lot of time away from home, though. But he always showed warmth. He always talked with his children and encouraged them.

HE OFTEN took his daughters swimming. And he sometimes took them fishing. Then, they drove to the neighboring fjords with their fishing rods. Straight to the pier and sea scorpions and other fish, small codfish took the bait. Sometimes they caught several and the cat got a treat.

"Mommy, you know what?" Erla María came in shouting and plunged through the door after one such trip. "We caught ten fish, Pjakkur our cat will be very happy." She continued, "Una caught two, I got five, and Daddy three." Her voice rang with joy and pride.

"Pjakkur, Pjakkur, where are you? Just come and see all the fish we caught for you."

Then Una came and I helped her take off her fishing clothes.

"Hello, my bunny Una, I heard that you caught two fish."

She nodded with pride in her eyes.

"This was really something, you caught all this fish. You're really good at fishing. You know, I have never caught a fish in my entire life. But you 're only four years old and you've already caught two."

She grew some inches, her smile was even wider, and said, "they're for Þjakkur."

Árni then entered the house, the last of them, carrying the rods and the catch, happy after a good day.

I WAS AT the post office, fetching something. We stood there, four persons, waiting. I waited at the first counter. Suddenly, a woman at the third counter called to me across the hall. I knew her vaguely.

"How is your husband doing?"

I looked at her.

"Is he seriously ill?" she continued.

This woman didn't understand what she was doing. She had no idea how she had phrased her question. Would she like to discuss her own private affairs publicly? It is possible to turn everything upside down. To degrade the other person just by the manner of asking. How do you know when people are showing sympathy or just satisfying their curiosity? I stood there on the post office floor and continued to watch the woman, trying to choose my response to her question. Most of all I wanted to tell her that my husband's health was none of her business.

"Yes, he is very ill. He's staying at Akureyri Hospital."

Then I thought, is he really very ill? Who says he is? Maybe he isn't ill at all. Maybe all this is just some nonsense. What did I just say? What words was I spreading for people to talk about in this community? Who's ill? Was he ill? At least he wasn't at work, so that meant he had to be ill.

DESIRE

The night is dark, almost black
Can new day rise up toward shore?
Am I now to end this track
Or is my light to shine once more?
It's a longing and wish for me
That pain was to quit its trance
And in the embrace of my family
To the future a one more chance

(Árni)

I WOKE UP to gales of laughter that came from the hallway. I had slept soundly this first night we spent at the Cancer Ward at Reykjavik Hospital. The laughter surprised me. Couldn't really believe that anyone was able to laugh in here, in this ward where the dead seriousness of life and death reigned. I didn't seem to realize that people are either alive or dead. There is a very distinct line between the two. Even though people are ill they still exist and can laugh and live in their own way. Yes, there was clearly laughter out in the hallway. This was Jón, a man from the countryside. A jovial guy, short and stocky, muscularly built. His blond hair had started to thin and he had a receding hairline.

He was cheerful, with a unique personality, using peculiar old-fashioned words when he spoke. He was around forty. He had been diagnosed with lung cancer, but it had spread all over the body, so there were small tumors in several organs, including his brain. He was married and had three-year-old triplets. I had seen his little fair-haired angels in beautiful hand-knit sweaters. They came to town, into the Cancer Ward, to visit their dad. Didn't understand what was taking place. The three of them ran giggling down the hallway.

I was so delighted to hear this laughter. Jokes flew around and there was lightness to life. Several tables had been arranged in a row in the corridor where breakfast was served. A breakfast buffet. This was like in a hotel. Jón was having breakfast. Joyful and open. He had a broken arm. Didn't complain. The fracture had prevented him from being at home for his own wedding. They were planning to get married and to confirm their love for each other with their small ones around them. But shortly before the wedding, he stumbled and fell on his hand and broke his upper arm. The fracture revealed a tumor in the bone that had caused it to snap.

"Thank you for waking me with this joyful laughter. I didn't know there was laughter in this ward," I said.

"Oh, sure, my dear, we most certainly laugh in here. We live by the principle of optimism and happiness. What else can we do?"

I was to have many conversations with Jón. He was a warm person. He sympathized with us. Sympathized with me. Was concerned about my husband. Though he was so very ill himself.

Later, when Árni was dead, I visited this ward. I had been to a meeting for those who had lost their spouse at the Cancer Ward, held at the hospital, and I wanted to come by and see the room where Árni had stayed. I saw Jón and his wife. Said hello to them. He was in a wheelchair. The illness was taking him. He was thinner and the color of his skin was familiar to me. I knew where he was going. But still, he was cheerful and happy. His eyes were alive. When I again visited the hospital, a few weeks later, I met a nurse in the entrance and asked her about Jón. She said he was still there. I got her permission to go and see him. He had just woken up from a deep sleep. He was on strong medication. I entered the room. I saw he was very ill.

"Jón," I said and took his hand.

"Do you remember me?"

He opened his eyes. It was as if it took him a short while to register the present and the place. Then suddenly, he seemed to come into this moment.

"Yes, of course I remember you."

"It's good to see you," I said.

"I remember so well how good it felt to hear your happy laughter and the joy you spread all over in this ward," I continued.

"Yes, but there isn't much of that here now. No, my dear, there is little joy around here now."

His eyes rolled in his head and it was as if he lost consciousness for a short moment. It took him a while to come back.

I felt it more clearly with each suffering individual I came close to, that life is only at each very moment. Nothing can budge life off the track of the moment but death. Jón died four days later.

Þór was already in the room when Árni was admitted to the Cancer Ward. A lean man. Dark-haired with dark stubble. It was obvious that he had quite an amount in the bank of experience. He was slim and had swift movements. Open and positive and ready to help us in any way he could. He had difficulty with speaking. He seemed to whisper. When I asked him where he had cancer he pointed at his throat and told me that the cancer had been found at the root of his tongue. Half of his tongue had to be removed.

I looked at him. Listened to him whisper. I don't know how I could keep my face without emotion while he told me this but it took me three days to recover from the shock of hearing his story. I couldn't think it through how it would feel to lose the tongue. I perceived so intensely the risk it took to be a human. Alive. Inside, I sensed a profound feeling of helplessness. A feeling that nothing can be taken for granted. I got a new feeling for my own tongue, examined it from various angles in the mirror. Saw the tears in my eyes and felt the pain and vulnerability in my chest.

I made good friends with Þór. He was around fifty, with a young wife and small children and adolescent children from his first marriage. He ran his own business and it was thriving. He sympathized with me. Wasn't too sure that Árni would recover. Gave my daughters sweets when they came for a visit. Two weeks later, when Árni had been moved to the Intensive Care, waiting for his death, I saw Þór. He was coming out of the hospital as I was entering. I watched him as he walked away from the building. I wanted to talk to him. But my voice betrayed me when I was going to call out. I didn't want to meet him to tell him how things were. I wanted to spare this man with cancer from hearing the news of another dying from the same disease. Þór lived a little over a year longer than Árni.

Then there was Jakob. He walked around wearing a green dressing gown, white hospital socks and slippers. He paced, kept on walking almost constantly, up and down the corridor. He had a fairly tinted skin. I sensed in him a man who had not had the privilege to be as most ordinary people are. To have the chance to join in and dance with the rest of us, the dance of life, establish a family, get education and make a career for himself. I sensed that he'd been standing on the sideline in life. Alone and on his own terms. He walked the corridors staring emptily ahead. He had rectangular pen marks in the upper area of his chest where his gown did not quite cover. Clear signs that he was in radiation therapy. It wasn't until my third day there that we started greeting each other.

He would say, "Good morning, I am recovering."

Then he would continue his walk, and meet me again on his way back.

"I feel I'm getting better. I'm feeling all better now."

In this small closed world in this ward, everyone seemed to look into each other. The need for sharing experience with others was great. To get to know people. But this need inherently held a conscious risk. The risk of losing newly found friends. Of being sucked into their suffering. Of pulling other people into your own suffering. But the need remained.

One day, I met Jakob in the sitting room. He sat down in a chair. We said good morning to each other.

"How are you today?" I said.

"I feel I'm getting better," he said, always using the same words.

He continued, "This is so odd. I just caught a cold, just an ordinary cold, like everyone else."

He looked out of the window, a distant gaze. He still seemed to wonder about this oddity of existence, that the cold he caught, just like anyone else, wasn't just an ordinary cold.

"I went to see the doctor because I didn't get better and then I was told I had lung cancer."

He looked at me again.

"I don't get it."

"I'm quite sure that there are a lot more people who have cancer without knowing it, "he continued.

And then he rose into his walk again through the endless corridors. I thought about his words, pictured in my mind's eye the next few dozen individuals coming into this ward. People who the author of life would select to discharge from this earthy existence. Jakob died a few months later.

Cancer Ward. It was our home now. Our younger daughters were fostered by relatives. Our oldest stayed with a friend of hers in Egilsstadir. How were they? I really didn't pause to think about it. I was experiencing much now and was hardly able to cope with all this new experience. I just "was" in my own existence through each day. You lay mostly in bed, sleeping. You had high fever that came, went and always returned again and again. Hundred-and-four. You were so hot and feverish and then came cold fits when you shivered intensely. A large man in a body that was getting smaller and smaller and had actually become too small for you. You shivered and your teeth rattled.

You were ice cold on the inside. Then the sweat attacks came. Your temperature rose and you lay drenched in sweat.

You were too weak to take a shower, leaning onto the IV stand with your right hand and my arm with your left. I often wondered what it would be like to be suffering from cancer, hairless, marked with the stamp of death, gliding through the corridors of this particular hospital ward. Meeting another human being who looks just like you, hairless, with the same stamp. Tottering with hope for life in your heart but anguish in the look of your eyes.

We walked the corridor. Never did go further than to the toilet. You walked slowly but carried yourself erect and with dignity. Never showed you suffered. Never gave in. This walk was a journey to the toilet and for washing. We found towels, washcloths and underwear. You sat down on the toilet for your needs that were hardly your private needs anymore because you needed support in everything you did. Your underwear fell loosely down your thin legs. Your legs that I always thought were exquisite. So gracefully shaped, even more feminine than my own. I watched your legs that were still so beautiful but so incredibly thin. Your knees pointed out into the air, bony, right out from your almost fleshless thighs. Where are you, the former you, whom I knew? Who is taking you away from me? You are disappearing! Slowly you stood up. I helped you take off your shirt. You were naked, ill, feeble and gaunt. Your skin also had a special color. Was it the color of the illness, the colour of death? I walked to the sink and moistened the washcloth with hot water. You sat down on the chair.

"Do you want me to do the washing or do you want to do it yourself?"

"Will you do it for me?"

I started at the top, the face, wiped your forehead and moved the cloth with care around your eyes. Wiped over your hairless cheeks. Some stubble was beginning to grow because you hadn't been on strong medication recently due to the fever. This high fever that came and went was the cause of less medication. Governed the medication. The stubble was alive. Newly grown and fresh. Peeking out from the hollow cheeks of your face. I moved the cloth up to the crown of your head where the hair was also beginning to peek up. I wondered if these hairs would be allowed to live or if they'd be killed with the next round of drugs.

Your back, it was clean and beautiful. The shoulder blades prominent. No spots. No blackheads. All were gone. Where had they gone to? I helped you lift up your arms and hold them up, so that I could wash your armpits.

"All right, love, now you can put on your shirt so you won't get cold. Then stand up so we can continue."

You stood up and I changed washcloths. This washing is memorable, a sign to me of your failing strength. A reminder that the illness was taking all of you away from me. I knelt down and washed your thighs; they were no thicker than the calves of my legs. I don't want this! I can't do this anymore! Who can be so horrible to harm us in this way? We have three daughters! They're waiting for us at home, waiting for us to come home and to become a family again my heart shouted. My mind answered, you're talking nonsense. There's nothing wrong with him. What you're experiencing now is not really happening. There's nothing particular going on and soon you will both go home together.

The washing over, my hands drew up your legs the smallest size of hospital underwear. Property of the National Hospital. You thanked me and sat down in the chair that was now placed in front of the mirror. Straight as an arrow, so handsome and with pure affection, you looked yourself in the eye in the mirror. How was he able to do this? What was he thinking? Was he giving thanks for the years he had been given? Did he look forward to leaving? I left him for a little while as I quickly stepped into the corridor and into the linen room where I was able to get a release for my emotions through tears and sobbing. Then I turned back and he sat and looked at himself still, in direct eye contact with his fate.

"All right, love, let's head back to our room."

And we stumbled back.

HE STOOD there in our hospital room. Introduced himself. The hospital priest, Larus. A man of average height, with a sturdy, muscular physique. Big blue eyes. Bright face. Smiled when he spoke. He talked to us directly and to the point with a gentle voice and in a slow manner. He held a Bible in his hands. Told us his name and then said, "I was passing by."

His handshake was firm and warm. We spoke for a little while.

"I will be coming by tomorrow. Would you like me to come and see you?"

We thanked him for the visit and told him that we would appreciate if he came by the next day. During the roughly two weeks that Árni stayed in the Cancer Ward, I got to know Larus quite well. He was warm and his embrace protective. He looked deep into my eyes and there seemed to be some part of eternity in his eyes. He smelled nice. He had the rare quality of being able to embrace me long and tight and yet, I didn't feel uncomfortable. He could sit for a long, long time, holding my hands in his, looking into my eyes, talking. Yet, he didn't say all that much. What he said was somehow neutral, yet explicit. As if he spoke from some higher point, without judgments, without pity, modest and did not preach. His words were memorable. He said that people would not change character by becoming ill. They would still remain the same, act the same, and react the same. Larus often showed up without notice. A bright, big bear with a warm embrace and the nice smell.

"Would you like me to stop for a moment now? I'll also be passing by tomorrow."

Larus was gentle and never welcomed himself on his own. Stood aside waiting. Met us where we were, as we were. He became my supporting pillar of life in this place. Made all the bad things a little better with his presence although he never opened the Bible. There was no need to. Our hope was in our hearts. Our fate was up to God or the Universe itself.

I WOKE UP; my sleep was shallow in this place. There was a constant coming and going of people. It was five in the morning. Someone was attending to Árni, nursing him, taking care of him and his needs. This someone was not me. I just slept and woke up when someone came and attended to him. A nurse. Where were we? Why did we sleep in separate beds, ice cold beds? We also seemed to sleep in some strange realm of time with our eyes shut and our senses numb, waiting for time to make its move in the chess game of life. It always did. It always had a stronger hand to play. We made our moves against it in our feeble effort. But we knew no tricky moves and were able neither to castle nor to check.

After the nurse had left I whispered, "Árni, are you awake?"

He said in a weak voice, "Yes."

"Árni, I must talk to you." I rose up in my bed. The lump in my throat thrust upwards and my eyes flooded.

"Árni, there are so many things I regret. I've been unfair so often. I often blamed you. I feel I haven't always been sincere enough in our relationship."

I talked and I cried. I don't remember now most of what I said. I just talked and cried.

"I forgive you all, Anna, I love you."

I fell silent and watched him. He just lay there. Linked to tubes, medication and needles.

"Árni, will you talk to me. I just want us to talk."

"I can't talk, not now, I'm so tired."

I stopped talking, put my toes on the floor and stepped out of my bed. Our beds were side by side with three feet of space in between. A chasm. An unbridgeable chasm. A chasm with a deep cold abyss. And the chasm was separating us.

Árni and I had often needed to jump over small fissures, sometimes even so deep that we needed to carefully master our leap. The hugeness of this chasm now, however, was such that we were unable to master the jump. No, we would now have to stand on each edge, meet eyes while the gap continued to increase, and finally the distance would be too great for our eyes to keep contact, and we would then only see the shape of each other. In the end, we would appear as some vague spots on the horizons.

I softly climbed out of bed, unable to sleep. I was emotionally upset. I cried. I ran into the nurse in the doorway. She hugged me and we walked out of the room. We went to the sitting room. She sat down in a chair and I sat in her lap. I'd become a little girl who wept. She was a hearty woman with a protective embrace. She didn't judge me, didn't take a defensive position. She was there, just having nursed my dying husband, and was now ready to care for me, the wife who would go on living. I don't know if she wept with me. I just know that I cried my heart out and made strange sounds. Sounds that I didn't recognize, but they came and I allowed them to come. We sat there together, sharing a moment that was not measured in time or space. A moment that contained us, two human beings, one in search of comfort, the other seeking to give comfort. A moment that was powerful and so memorable that it is still crystal clear in my heart.

The significance of personal belongings changes. Glasses and a watch of a dying man. These are different to view on a shelf or on a table than glasses or a watch belonging to someone who has just gone to take a shower. It's as if the nature of the absence of the owner changes the observer's perspective to these things. When he was moved from the Cancer Ward for the third and last operation, I stood alone in his sick room. His hospital bed was rushed to the operating room. Everything was bleeding. Life was ebbing away.

I stood there alone, looked at the empty space where the bed had been. I saw your watch and your glasses lying on the table where you had put them. I looked at these two things that belonged to you. Lying there but you were gone. Personal belongings that were a part of your everyday life. Aided you in your everyday needs. Would you ever again put on your glasses? Or the watch on your wrist? Who could answer that? Probably you would not touch them again. I walked to the desk and took up the watch. Rolled it between my fingers. Observed the inside of the strap and noticed the darker colour of the leather where it had lain against your skin. And the glasses, these beautiful glasses that looked so good on you. It wasn't long since you'd bought them. Still, the paint had begun to fade just a little on the temple arch on the right side. I held these objects in my hands and looked right through them.

A family meeting was to come with our oldest daughter, Addy, twelve years old. The other two were too young. She was coming by plane from Egilsstadir. I had wished that she'd chosen to arrive last night. Árni had been in especially good form then. Our two younger ones had come to see him. They hadn't seen him for two or three days. But yesterday they came and sat on my bed that stood beside his. Little girls in their beautiful dresses, presents from their aunt, sitting on a hospital bed, dangling their legs in the air and telling their daddy some jokes. We smiled and laughed. He seemed to have enough strength to laugh with them and encourage them.

"Daddy, do you know why people in Hafnarfjordur always take a ladder with them to the store?"

"No, I don't."

"Because the price is so high."

When it was time to go they climbed to the head of his bed and kissed him good-bye. I then took them to their grandmother's. Planned to stay there myself overnight. Didn't know that this would be his last night there.

He'd begun to bleed this same morning. At first it wasn't pure blood. I noticed it myself because I helped him relieve himself into a blue tray for vomit. Nothing came as a surprise anymore. Anything could happen. And last night had been difficult. Continuous internal bleeding. Blood accumulated in his abdomen, which then became swollen. Until his abdomen didn't have room for more. Then it forced its way up and through his mouth. Clean and fresh blood that ought to be flowing in your veins sought a way out of your body. Wasn't part of the circulation anymore. The circle was coming to an end. As if it were a long-distance runner who suddenly decided that now it was time to stop running after running the same lap so often. The circle was broken. And there was no return to life again. Your blood gushed out warm into the cold air where blood cannot survive. It's just at the very moment of its flowing while it is blood-red and beautiful, emitting its unique sense of freshness. The instant it comes into contact with something else it turns into a blot that does nothing but cake and darken. Die.

The next destination was the Intensive Care. There he lay in bed. More sick than ever. The doctors had told me when I came this morning that he had had incessant internal bleeding all night. And always this high fever, hundred and four.

"We've given him 25 bottles of blood in twelve hours, which almost immediately returns out through his mouth. We cannot continue to give him blood at this rate. His body cannot handle it much longer and The Bank of Blood will soon put a stop to us."

"We must operate on him and find out what's causing this internal bleeding," the oncologist said.

"This is a difficult operation and we don't know if he will survive it."

I felt a growing frenzy inside. Was he supposed to have a third operation? And then what? *And then what*? This had to stop.

I put aside the watch and the glasses. My daughter was here already and the meeting was about to start. There were only two of the family who were here. The mother and the oldest daughter, along with the oncologist, the priest and the social worker. The daughter was silent. Sensed how things had turned. Knew what was happening. She'd told me that she'd rather that her daddy would be allowed to die than suffer anymore. Sensitive. Shy. Regretful that she hadn't arrived the day before. We were in the sitting room. There wasn't much to say. I was the one who talked the most. And what could the others say to a child whom they didn't know at all? A girl they were meeting for the first time? A child who had come here to say her last good-bye to her father?

"He needs to go through an operation that's both big and difficult. And we don't know if he will survive." These were my words.

"He has been so dear to us," I continued, "so strong, but now he's very ill."

Our daughter wept.

"I know," she said, and kept on weeping.

"And we have much to be thankful for. Now, we don't have any other choice than to face this. We don't want to see him suffer more."

"No," she said.

"And you've been so strong yourself. Staying away from us at your friend Anna's and her family. Playing soccer. Playing for your dad. He's so proud of you. You couldn't have done anything that was better for him. He loves you so much." I didn't say more.

Sometimes words do more harm than good. In difficult times they must be few and well chosen.

Everyone was numb. We, the mother and the daughter, were dealing with a situation that would have a permanent impact on our future. The others were at work. I wondered how many meetings like this they held every month. How many dying eyes did they look into in their jobs?

The meeting was over. Nothing more to say. We hugged, those of us who wanted to; the rest shook hands or exchanged looks.

The sun was shining. Everything was so beautiful and bright in the sun. The houses, the cars, the trees and the children playing outside. Why does everything look so much brighter and more beautiful when the sun shines? Why wasn't my Árni in the sun? Why did he lie in there with the curtains drawn?

He lay there. We walked to his bed. Father and daughter looked at each other in anguish. His face was deformed by the edema that had accumulated on his body in great quantities during the past four days. His eyes were sunken. Deep down in them I saw agony. The time to say good-bye had come. We knew.

"It's so good to see you, love," he said to her.

"Dearest daddy," she said.

Our eyes were wet with tears. I stepped aside to let them be alone for a while. Watched her stand, bend over her father and kiss him. Say some words to him. A girl in her early teens. She would never be the same. She said good-bye to him. Wished him good luck. Then walked back to me. I hugged her tightly and then walked over to his bed. My husband's bed. I stood where she had stood just a moment earlier, our girl. I bent slightly over him and looked into his eyes. These eyes I knew so well, but hardly knew now. Eyes that had watched me during our life, met mine. Eyes that had many facets. Eyes that knew me so well. Your smiling eyes. Yes, you always smiled with your eyes. You had funny smiling wrinkles under your eyes that grew deeper as you got older. But the eyes I now looked into were anxious. This last time was hard. It was the hardest.

"My dearest love, my best friend." I kissed him on his forehead. His hot forehead. "We must hope for the best." I dried a small drop of tear that crept from his eye.

"It'll be fine," he said.

"I have so much to thank you for. Thank you for all your gifts." I said this. "Good luck." I bent over him and kissed his lips caked with his dried blood. Then he was wheeled to the operating room.

Our daughter and I hugged each other and cried.

"We must hope for the best," I said.

"Yes, Mommy."

We walked into the waiting room. Looked out of the window. It was our National Day, 17th of June. People were dressing up for the day and on their way to celebrate downtown. Balloons, pinwheels and smiling faces in the sunshine of our National Day.

Five hours later, it was still the National Day of Iceland. The sun smiled to the children on the streets of Reykjavík and we were still at the hospital, my daughter and I. Did we go somewhere while Árni was being operated on? I can't remember. At least we were there now. *Now* was a particular point in time that indicated some direction.

Now was that time. How often hasn't one experienced a particular *now*? There always is a specific now. And now we were waiting for the doctor. The operation was over.

Árni's mother, his brothers and sisters and their spouses were present as well. We sat in the family waiting room. Silent. A candle on the table. Refreshments. Some juice, coffee and biscuits. Two doctors entered the room. The oncologist and an anesthetist. They took seat with us.

"Well, the operation is over," the oncologist spoke.

"Unfortunately, we were unable to find the location of the bleeding," he continued.

"What do you mean, you didn't find where all this blood came from?" I asked.

"No, I'm sorry, we couldn't."

"Why is that?" I asked.

"When a patient has been operated on, the organs react to external stimuli with contraction of the veins and then there is no way to see where the bleeding comes from." It was the anesthetist who explained by holding one of his palms open and touching it with the other hand. With the touch the palm instantly closed. Didn't yield.

"What does this mean? Won't he start bleeding again?"

"Yes, the bleeding will begin again."

I rose.

"And what are you going to tell him? Are you just going to tell him that you didn't find anything?!" It was me who yelled.

"That's impossible! He must never hear this! He cannot take it! He doesn't want to hear it!"

No one said a word for a while. Life tore through me. My blood was racing through my veins and I couldn't do anything. I just stood there and reacted to the words that had just cracked the air.

The oncologist stroked his chin. Prepared his words with special care. He wasn't in an easy position.

"The fact is that we have come to an end. We're unable to control the situation. We're losing him. We haven't got the means to cure him. We were able to see that the cancer has spread. It has spread to the stomach as well. This type is prone to spreading to the brain. He would live for three more months, at the most."

The anesthetist took over. "He will receive palliative treatment. He won't need to wake up, but will be kept in a deep sleep, so he won't suffer. He's connected to a respirator."

"And how long will this take?" I asked.

"He will live for two to three days."

There was nothing as real as this cold present that was taking place. The outcome of this game was decided. There was no more fending off. No illusory hope could warm the hearts beating in the chests of the patient's family. Hearts that were about to break over the circumstances of the pending present.

We, your family, all walked slowly into the room where you lay sleeping. Your sister and her husband were home from abroad. For some reason their flight had been cancelled. They were supposed to have arrived yesterday. They didn't get to look into your eyes. We walked into your room and you lay there in a deep sleep. You lay on your back and breathed through the machine that pumped the air in and out with a loud, rhythmic sound. Asleep. Ready to die. Ready to leave us. You wouldn't wake up to life again. Some instruments were connected to you. The nurse explained their necessity. The oncologist explained how you received medication through the instruments.

"He will get very strong medication and will not feel any pain. He will only sleep very deeply. And we won't set up any nutrition for him."

We formed a protective shield around your bed. Crying. We stood in the middle of this reality that we didn't want. And you lay there on your back. Peaceful. The nurse said that it was time to give you more medication. She called your name, "Árni!"

You answered by lifting your eyebrows. You were obviously about to wake up. But you mustn't do that. The nurse's task was to make sure that you would by no means wake up. If you did then you would feel so much pain because of the large incision on your stomach. It went from your chest down to your groin. No, it would be best that you slept. For us as well, so we didn't have to look into your eyes. Wouldn't have to share these facts about your life. And I wouldn't have to see the regret in your eyes over leaving me alone with everything. Our daughters. Raising them. Our business. The income. The life we had chosen to spend together. All of this would be in my hands from now on. Our plans. In my hands. On my shoulders. Best that you slept.

"Yes, he's clearly gaining consciousness. It's time to increase the dose."

She had already prepared it. It was in a small syringe that was attached to a very thin tube connected to your body. She changed the syringe. Strong medication in a small syringe.

You never lifted your eyebrows again. You didn't just live for three days. You lived for eight days. I sat with you almost all of this time and also in the family waiting room. Your relatives usually filled up the room. They took turns sleeping there. I went home every night to get rest. I needed that. Took a sleeping pill. A half one. I, who detested sleeping pills. Took them now. That's how my life was. I couldn't help it.

You were peaceful. Just lay there and slept. Breathed. You didn't hold the reins anymore in this life. You were headed in a different direction.

I then went down the Cancer Ward to pick up your things. Your clothes and shoes. Your watch and glasses. These things had now served their purpose. The purpose to serve you while you needed them. And now this wasn't so anymore. Now they didn't serve a purpose. They were put in the exact same bag as they were in when they'd arrived. Your bag. That was now my bag. I spoke with the nurses. They asked about you.

"Is there anything new?"

"He's sleeping. He's dying. That's how it turned. But he doesn't feel any pain. He looks peaceful and beautiful. You should go and see him. I'm so grateful to you. You took such good care of him."

I hugged them good-bye. They were wonderful persons who had chosen to work in a place like this. Witnessing the suffering of other people every day. They were ordinary, wonderful women. Women, who had families, went to the movies, to the theatre and lived their ordinary lives in between shifts.

THE DAYS passed slowly in the Intensive Care. You had so much fluid in your body that you were in no hurry to die. You took your time. You became more and more beautiful as the edema disappeared. I sat with you and whispered so many things in your ear. I was certain that you heard everything I said. All kinds of thoughts and memories came to mind. I sat with you and held your hand. It was hot and gave me warmth but it didn't answer my hand. It was asleep. As if it were dead. It would never squeeze my hand again. It would never touch my breasts again. It stayed with you, this hand, and belonged to the life you lived. Always had. Your beautiful, artistic hands. They rested there in peace. I wrote a poem.

Your mouth I know so well
Was caked with blood
Dry and open
Your hands that cuddled me
Lay lifeless
Motionless
Hot
Your hands that will
Never again
Caress me
Your mouth that will
Never again
Kiss my lips

YOU WERE still bleeding. The blood trickled from you through a tube that was inserted in your stomach and connected to a plastic bag that was fastened down by the side of your bed. Your blood flowed from life to death. I took the tube and held it in my palm. The blood was still warm. I got to touch the last heat, the last warmth of your blood. The remains of your life, in my hands. Trying to keep them warm. Trying to let them give me warmth. Your blood that preserved all of your life now flowed from you and got cold as soon as it entered the bag. All the effort you had made. All that you fought for. All that you envisioned.

Your life
Ebbing away
Your blood
Gushes
From your body
Slips through my palms
Into the grip of death
It is there now
Cold
So cold
And I
Living flesh
Living breath

Where will life lead me
Where will I lead life

I sat with you. Doomed to live. Forced to go on living. To go through this. To fight. Thoughts and memories flowed into my mind. I felt deep grief. Deep pain. But also deep joy. Indescribable joy. Such joy as I had never felt before. And I also thought my inner depth was infinite. It was as if there was a well in there. A well of wisdom that quenched my thirst. That brought me joy in my grief, filled me with joy where I sat and was losing you. Watching you die. It felt good to sit by your side. You were peaceful. I wondered if you had known for long how things would end. I always thought you wouldn't live to be old. And that's how it went.

This was Árni's seventh day in a coma. They had said he wouldn't live more than three. Now he needed stronger and stronger doses of anesthetics. And the type of drug had been changed two or three times because his body didn't seem to be able to process more than a certain dose of each drug before it would stop working.

I picked up the phone. I was in the doctor's office in the Intensive Care. I was about to call Árni's internist in Akureyri. I needed to get news about Árni's condition but I wasn't able to reach his doctor here in Reykjavík. That's why I called the one in Akureyri.

"Hi, Anna. Is there anything new? Any change?" he asked.

"No, he's in the same condition. It takes such a long time. He's so strong. Is there a possibility to disconnect the respirator?"

"Anna, this so difficult. A friend of mine in United States go through this. He be sick in heart and stay in respirator. And machine was turned off. Not allowed in Iceland. But I know Árni do not want it this way."

I listened to his words through the telephone. His voice that came from another location in Iceland. Why couldn't he be here?

"Anna, respirator is only to keep alive in him. He can't live if it's disconnected. He not want this kind of life. But it's difficult. Icelandic rules not allow to disconnect."

I started crying.

"This is such a hard day. He just goes on living. And now I've got only one wish left for him. I wish that he can die. But I wish he wouldn't need to take all these drugs and wouldn't need to be connected to this machine that pumps life into him when the only thing he has left is to die."

"I wish I could be with you," he said.

"Thank you."

We talked some more about the respirator and I told him I was going to discuss this with the doctors.

"Yes, do that and let me hear then."

I walked into the family waiting room where his mother and brother-in-law were. I told them about my phone call to Akureyri and the possible option of disconnecting the machine, but explained the different rules in Iceland and the United States. I said I wanted to look into this option. I wanted us to consider it and discuss it with the doctors. What better thing could be done for a dying man? Was there a greater gift for him than the freedom from this life? The freedom to die?

We held a meeting. Árni's mother, his brothers and sisters, their spouses, his aunts and uncles and me. We discussed the issue from various angles. I was raging inside. Something had to be done. It was as if there we were trying to interrupt the preordained process life itself had chosen. The doctors had expected him to die three days ago. It was as if life had betrayed us. Or was it death? Here we gathered together to discuss if it was an option to make a life shorter. If it was within our power. Supporters of death. I, who always had been supporting life. Why didn't we trust life to support itself? Why did we sit here now talking about this? Did we have authority over life? Over death?

We called for a doctor and told him what we were thinking. He appeared, a warm man, wearing a white doctor's coat. Slightly built, with a bright appearance. Greyish hair and glasses. He looked deep into the eyes of those he spoke to. He was equal to us and modest. Sat down with us. A man who had been close to death more often than most, because of his work. An anesthetist in the Intensive Care, who'd rarely had the chance to look into his patients' eyes or to hear them speak. Most often he'd hear their groans. Most certainly, he'd never heard them laugh. Never saw them at their best, not in this ward. He treated chronically ill bodies whose eyes were shut. Bodies that suffered because life kept them alive, some of which would return to life, others not.

It was I who began, "We would like to discuss if there is a possibility of disconnecting the respirator. He just goes on living and is in need of all this strong medication. It's so hard to watch him become immune to more and more drugs. This isn't a life. Isn't it possible to make it easier for him?"

The doctor answered, "We treat him in what we consider to be the best way. Yes, you're right, this takes a long time. Árni is strong. He has a healthy heart, lungs and kidneys. We didn't assume that he might live this long. I remember only a handful of cases where we've had to administer such strong doses of medicine as we do for him. But the Icelandic rules do not allow a respirator connected to a patient to be disconnected. That is only allowed in the case of brain death."

Brain death. My God, this was a horrible term. Brain death. I couldn't picture a dead brain within a living body. Somehow, I just wasn't able to understand this. I was placed in a world where I neither knew nor understood many of the concepts that were used, and didn't understand what was behind them.

"What do you mean?

"I mean when the cerebral function has stopped. It's only allowed in such cases. Nor does Icelandic law permit the patient's family to have an influence on when his life is to be ended. It's in the hands of specialists to assess any given situation. The relatives are never called upon to participate in such a decision. The duty of each doctor is to provide a patient with the best palliative treatment possible when medical treatment has been stopped. This can be done with medication and the aid of equipment, such as the respirator in this case, so that the patient won't have to suffer. Árni isn't conscious and is in a deep sleep."

I felt better after this meeting. I wasn't myself steering you into death, away from me and our daughters. You were you; you were alive. People are either alive or dead. There is nothing in between. I sat beside you. Whispered in your ear. Wept by your side. Enjoyed anointing your face with my tears. I watched your body shrink. Your stubble grow. Your cheeks become more and more hollow. But you remained there, listening to me. Your hand alive, hot and soft, covered mine if I let it. I sometimes did, let it hold mine. I would slip my hand under yours and feel it wrap mine, heavy and warm. I let it support me in the life that was ahead for me. Without you. On my own with our daughters. Who would hold my hand when yours became cold? But it was not cold. Not yet. It was still there warm and tender. Your blood had stopped flowing in small streams into the bag. It wasn't really any blood now, but dark lumps that formed blotches inside the tube and then ended in the bag. They were separated from the fluid that was in the bag and also came from your body. Bodily fluid. It was all somehow separated. I would never again look into your eyes. I didn't dare to lift your eyelid and look. I didn't want to see it open and asleep. Open and dying. I wanted to remember your eyes alive, looking at me.

I was in the midst of a reality I didn't know; an alien reality that was absolute. I couldn't escape it. It flooded all over us, turned us into new individuals. An unreal reality. My dreams were more real. They were familiar, led me to places that I knew. With you. There we held hands. Both of us alive. Bright and beautiful. Determined to carry out all the things we had longed to do but never did, determined to leave nothing behind. To take off on our family vacation, the one we had already planned and had booked just before you got ill. To work less, spend more time together. To build the house as we'd planned and move into it. Our business had started to show some profit around the time you were diagnosed.

It was good to be able to vanish into my dreams. Maybe you were also dreaming with me. Where was your mind right now? Where was your soul? I often looked under your duvet to see your feet. They lay there still, waiting. They waited for what was about to come. To become cold. I touched the soles that would never again touch a floor. They wouldn't take more steps on this earth. Was it I who led you the last steps? I don't know. I hope so. Some big dark spots had begun to show on the back of your heels from lying motionless in the same position for so long. It was as if the blood from your still toes had sunken down your feet to the back of your heels. Awaiting heels. And similar spots also on other parts of your body, on your elbows and at the nape of your neck. I felt as if your body had started to ruin. The thought of it was uncomfortable. I felt uneasy looking at these spots and wanted to rinse them off your body. I felt that you shouldn't have to go through this too. I felt enough was enough, but I could do nothing, just sit by your side and thank you for your life with me. The life we lived together and which I sometimes thought of as difficult. But we also had good moments and moments of deep happiness. Yes, quite a few. And now, when I put both good and bad times on the scale, the good ones turned out to be far more numerous. That was how I felt now. They were profound and gave back joy and thankfulness. The hard times left me with lessons learned. I was in the school of life, sat in the front row.

I DIDN'T DARE to a look at the incision after the last operation. I felt weak from just the thought of how recently you had been operated on. An incision cut right through another one. No, I couldn't bear to think about it. Yet I did. I tried to get rid of the thought. Let you be covered by the duvet all the time. I was careful never to push my hand on your body, to make sure you would endure no pain from the weight of my hand that was enclosed in yours on the duvet. The nurse told me that the functions of your body would focus on centralizing, that the actual bodily function in your outer limbs had ceased. It was now mainly centered on the organs in your torso, without limbs. There your strongest organs were fighting. Heart, lungs and kidneys. Odd. I'd never even given it a thought that some bodies died this way. Never. Knew nothing about this. Really didn't know much. By discovering something new in life you realize of how little you really know.

❀

WHEN IS there a moment of farewell? When is the right time to say good-bye? Does the moment of farewell belong to both persons? Do you say good-bye to your spouse who is still alive when you know he's dying? Or will you do it after his death? The one who loses her spouse from a sudden death will say good-bye after he's dead. I think there is not just one moment of saying good-bye, whatever the circumstances of death. I think we say good-bye again and again and mostly within our hearts. We enjoy many meetings with the beloved in our heart, whether he's seriously ill or dead and the moments of bidding farewell are numerous. During Árni's illness many moments of good-bye appeared in our daily lives.

At some point I said good-bye to Árni as a lover, when I knew that we would never make love again. At some I said good-bye to him as a partner in my daily life when it was clear that he would never come back home from the hospital. At some point I said good-bye to him as a healthy individual who would go off to work and on the way home drop by in the store to buy groceries. At some point I said good-bye to him as my parent partner raising our daughters and a participant in our family life. Our moments of saying good-bye became more frequent. His chances to survive were less and less and finally they were limited to lying in bed, breathing. When he went to the last operation I said good-bye to his eyes. I suspected that I would never look into them again. But I didn't say that to him, I said good-bye to his eyes in my heart. Gradually I came to say good-bye to his body lying connected to the respirator. I sat with him all day long, went out to have something to eat or to get fresh air.

❀

THE DAY he died, we were, many of us, with him; his mother, his brothers and sisters and their spouses. We, the women, went out for a breath of fresh air and took a walk up to The Church of Hallgrimur. It was around two o'clock. A priest was giving a sermon to a group of seniors. We sat down quietly on the bench to find relaxation. Then one of our phones rang. The hour had come. Árni had died just while we had gone out for a moment. It was odd, but then I had a moment of saying good-bye to him in my heart, there in the church. I was glad that I had been in there when he died, not in a shopping mall or yet another place. When we came back to the hospital he had turned white. His skin had started to get cold but he was still warm beneath it. I said good-bye to him again, pure white as he was.

Afterwards, we had a moment of prayer. There was no priest available in the hospital at this moment so I said the prayer myself. We stood together, the family, forming a protective circle around him, my newly dead husband, and I said the prayer over him. It sprang from my mouth as if coming from a deep well. I don't remember now what I said or how I did it, but I do remember that I spoke from a well of deep wisdom that was within me. Not that I spoke words of wisdom, but there as I was saying good-bye to my husband I experienced a deep, serene moment, the most profound moment of my life. The words seemed to speak themselves out of my mouth. It was a pure moment of peace, this last one, connected with death. We ended by saying the Lord's Prayer, I think. There we all said good-bye to Árni.

Suddenly, my Árni had become a corpse. He was now just a cold and stiff body and his physical remains were lying in a cold storage room somewhere in the Reykjavik

Cemeteries. Now, it was all over but his dead body needed to be prepared for the coffin The priest brought up the subject with me; would I like to take part in dressing Árni's body? I had never been so closely exposed to the presence of death as now. I had seen my aged grandmother lying in her coffin when I was a child, and I was twenty-five when my father died after a short and sudden illness, lying at a respirator for two weeks beforehand. I did not attend to his dead body in any way. So when the priest mentioned this I was taken aback. In fact, I answered him before I had thought the matter through. Suddenly, I had already told him that I did not feel up to doing it and at this moment I felt uneasy with the thought. I felt that his body was so gaunt and damaged that I did not find the strength to manage to participate in preparing him for the coffin. But I was soon to regret my decision, when it was too late to react and take part in it and my regret became more disturbing as time passed. I would have wanted my hands to be the very last hands to touch his body before he was put into the coffin.

Three years later I received the gift of dressing the dead body of an aged friend of mine. We had been close friends and confidants for several years. He showed me great compassion and support during Árni's illness and after his death. My old friend knew what he wanted to wear when he was to come to say good bye to this world and he had asked me long before to buy these clothes. A pair of long-sleeved silk underwear and I also bought a special soap as he wished me to wash them before he would be dressed in them. His relatives did not know about these wishes. When he died, at the age of ninety-five, I relayed his wishes to them and the location of the underwear. I washed them by hand and dried them and then had the honour to dress my dead old friend in these clothes for his last journey. This was a remarkable experience for me; I thought of Árni and in my mind I dressed his body. I accepted my regret that I had not done the same for him.

There's a sharp distinction between being alive and being dead. During Árni's palliative treatment everything was so tender, time just floated by. Every breath was audible, until all suddenly became silent. Then, the cold, hard reality took over. Death certificate. Closing accounts. Sending out notices that Árni wasn't alive any longer. Talking to a priest. Finding hymns. Writing Árni's life summary. Arranging for his body to be transported to the east, to our village Egilsstadir. Thus, life became cold and hard, although it was the middle of summer with bright sunshine in a blue sky. That was unbelievable.

There was a ceremony of laying the body of Árni in the coffin. Many relatives came and this was their moment of saying farewell. I don't remember all that much from this ceremony. It took place in Reykjavík and the hospital priest took care of it. It was the most odd day as our ceremony was in the morning and in the afternoon I attended the funeral of the father of my sister's son. This meant that both the fathers of all my mother's grandchildren were dead. I had never before attended a ceremony of laying a body in the coffin and a funeral in the very same day. Our ceremony was traditional, with the closest family present. Our daughters had drawn pictures and written some words for their father that they laid in his coffin along with a red rose. I had also written a letter to Árni that I placed inside. This moment was difficult and it was hard to watch his mother and grandparents saying their last good-bye to a young man, surviving him. It was so much not the correct order.

With the funeral in the church in Egilsstadir, the crowd of friends and family bade Árni farewell. His funeral was a profound moment in our lives. His last assignment had been to work on the design and layout of the book History of Egilsstadir. It was in printing when he lay ill and just before he died he was given a copy of the book on his sickbed. The day of his funeral was the 50th anniversary of Egilsstadir and also the publishing day of the book. The whole community celebrated. It was midsummer. So this day was both a day of grief and of joy for many inhabitants of our town. Árni had been the director of the sports association Hottur for several years. Its members stood in two lines outside the church to honor him when the funeral was over. They all dressed in the union's uniforms and it was very festive to watch them.

The ceremony itself was beautiful. The priest in Egilsstadir conducted it. The leaflet with the funeral program was especially designed by an employee at our business, deep blue with bright yellow dandelions. Dandelions were also used for decoration at the funeral feast. Bright yellow in bowls of water. Several girlfriends of our oldest daughter sang a song from the children's church program. It was very moving. Árni's younger brother, a composer, had written a song dedicated to his memory and performed it on a grand piano in the church. I had meant to talk to the young man and ask him to sing the song "I live in a dream," but it so happened that the song writer himself was visiting the east of Iceland at the time. Árni's brother is well acquainted with him and asked him to sing his song at the funeral, which he did.

This was a deeply moving ceremony for me. I didn't shed tears, but I was in a strange place within myself. It was odd to sit in the front row and to witness all this finiteness. I was saying good-bye to the one who had played the main role in this play and now at the funeral I had become the main actress. We then went to the cemetery because Árni had wished to be buried in Egilsstadir instead of his home village on the south. He had mentioned to me that I shouldn't tie myself down to his grave. He wanted me to be free from him, to live my own life. The coffin was lowered into the grave after everyone had made their sign over it. It was the final earthly moment with Árni. The very last good-bye. And then, there was the wake, the first gathering of his family and friends without him. A turning point. Our friends and neighbors had baked cakes and made some gourmet dishes. There was much warmth and friendship that met us in our small community. I felt the community was our family. There was a table affluence with food and drink and I cannot describe my gratefulness for these gestures. Many guests had come a long way. Old friends of Árni, some of whom I had never met before. I shook hands with all, I think, and I've never before or since received so many hugs in one day. I was happy with the day and did shine in some peculiar way.

Now, many more moments of good-byes came, and they all took place in my heart. They were of all kinds, some tainted with anger, especially in the beginning, but as time passed, gratitude filled the space. The good thing about the "heart" good-byes is that you can create them yourself. I was able to decide what I said to Árni, to thank him for the gifts he gave me as a human being, and when I did, I became sensitive, emotional and tender. I could meet him in my heart and promise him that I would do the best I could to be a good parent. That was the most important issue for me.

Many came to visit just after Árni died and there were myriad flowers all over in our house. Our relatives, who had come for the funeral and stayed at some of our friends' houses, now returned to their homes. The phone rang a lot these days and I was still in a strange state of euphoria in the sweet fragrance of flowers. Then, the flowers wilted and their smell turned bad. I threw them away and slowly the everyday routine took over in our house. Silent and empty. Hollow, the same as I was. I often filled it up with music. Then, the girls came home from kindergarten and school and filled the house with happiness and life and daily chores. Outwardly, life was again on its ordinary course. Inwardly, chaos and grief still reigned. Days and weeks passed and it became less frequent to hear the phone ring.

I CAME TO realize that for some it was hard to lose a friend and it was hard to watch the vulnerability of his spouse. I sometimes found it uncomfortable when people paid me attention too "eagerly" and at the same time, I felt that some people "easily could have" been more often in contact with us.

I want to relate an incident that shows how a grieving friend, witnessing my vulnerability as a surviving spouse, reacted in an extreme manner in his attempt to be of help. This was a friend of mine who was always very kind to us and still is. This man has been a true friend to me and supportive ever since we first met. He was our good friend and he is a good friend of mine today, keeps up, calls us and pays us a visit every now and then. He asks for news of our daughters, and has given a helping hand when I have made major decisions in my life. I'm very happy to have the chance here to thank him for that.

It was Sunday morning. I woke up late. He had come for a visit. Our friend; my friend. My brother-in-law and his wife were staying at my house with their young daughter. They hadn't visited us for a long time and now they were staying for two nights. I hadn't slept well. I'd been up writing the night before. Weeping. I didn't fall asleep until three o'clock and now I was out of shape and getting up to make coffee for my friend, something I didn't feel like doing at this moment. Would rather have rested longer in bed. My little girls were watching the morning cartoons on TV. The youngest one wasn't in the best of moods, and I could sense that my patience was short. I attended to her needs but I was irritated and let it show. I didn't feel like talking to my friend now. I didn't say it explicitly but tried to make him understand how I felt. Still, I thought that one "shouldn't" behave this way. Of course, you're supposed to be polite. But I had somehow had too much of his presence and wanted to have some time without him.

He sat down at the kitchen table as he always did. Always took the same seat. It's the same with all guests; it's how all of us choose our seats. We always prefer the same chair, sitting in the same place. We'd rather always do the same thing and we find it absurd to try something new. We wouldn't take a new seat unless our old chair was missing. We keep to a secure space without pretexts. We don't adopt new behavior unless we're forced to. We seldom take the initiative to make changes. We sit in the same seat, eat from the same plate, the same kind of bread. We drink the same coffee. We adopt a routine and do the same things at the same times. We watch the same surroundings. We keep company with the same people. We stick to our old views, using the same words. We only do what we are familiar with. We keep on repeating the same clichés day in, day out. Until some major event occurs in our life. Sometimes it's a joyful event. It can be something horrible. And we're thrown against a wall and placed there, with our back against it. We must face unfamiliar facets of life. The things we knew and were accustomed to don't have that familiar appearance anymore. Nor are we the same. We're not the same people we used to be. Then and only then do we cease to care what chair we take. And the old cliché doesn't have the same taste anymore. Everything is new. Everything has changed.

He sat there in his chair looking at me with a peculiar expression of pity on his face.

"You're so tired," he said.

"Mommy, I want to eat here in the living room," my youngest one called.

"Honey, you know I want you to eat in the kitchen," I called back.

"You don't look good," he continued.

"Mommy, please come?"

I walked into the living room. Why couldn't they just sit there and watch TV without wanting me to wait on them and give them attention? I just didn't have anything to give this morning with the visitor in the kitchen who had dragged me out of my warm bed. What was his business, coming here a hundred times a day? Was he just checking on me to make sure that I was this way or the other? That I was okay? Assuring himself that I wasn't all right and that I desperately needed him? That was the case, I thought. That I couldn't do without him and he wished to have a special place in my life. He wanted to be my main supporter, carry me in his arms, vulnerable as I was.

I returned from the living room.

"You look so tired," the friend said one more time.

I stopped in front of him, as I came through the doorway. Watched him and stamped down my foot while I said the words. "Shut up."

The words came with great a force, from deep within.

Shocked, he sat stiff in his chair. Had a new look in his eyes. Something new and unfamiliar had happened. Something that changed the existence in one second.

"How do you come to think it's your business the way I look?" I continued. "Am I in some beauty contest, or what? I was up and awake until three in the morning, crying. Who do you think looks pretty after such a night? I don't care one bit about how others think I look. I may have eye-bags down to my knees without having other people meddling with that and worrying about me. I can't stand it when people talk about how I look and how they say it. Who do you think I am? A victim? I'm not a victim. I've never felt that way and I'm fully capable of taking care of myself. I just have to tell you that I can't stand you coming here three times a day. Why can't you behave towards me like you did before? In the past weeks you've been making comments about how I look and warning me that some drooling men might start to come prowling around my house, waiting. I can't stand your meddling. It's none of your business what I do and whom I might choose to see. If I want to sleep with a man, tomorrow or whenever, I will do so without asking you. I can't stand it when someone tells me what to do. I'm perfectly capable of making my own choices. I don't need anyone to decide for me. And I can't stand you coming here all the time."

The words poured out of my mouth; they kept coming in a relentless stream. They placed themselves between us and changed our circumstances and our relationship. He sat in the same chair. A changed man. My words were like a stabbing with a knife. He lay fatally wounded, had no words himself. Knew now that old worn clichés had become distasteful. Unacceptable.

"I am concerned about you," he stammered.

"I watch this little family, so dear to me, having lost so much. I want so much to be of help. I don't treat you any differently than before."

He talked. Said some words. But wasn't sure. Was bewildered, unfamiliar to himself in a new place. The chair didn't even give him security.

"It isn't normal you coming here three times a day," I continued. "Taking your coffee breaks from work, here."

I rested my back against the kitchen counter. I couldn't bear the thought of sitting down at the same table as him. As though if I did, I would fall into his story. I wanted to stick to my own. My side of the story. I had to stick up for myself. I couldn't approach him. I just had to somehow tell him off. Talk about his awkwardness, though I knew it grew from meaning well. All his good and kind acts towards me were now transforming into some absurd nonsense.

Then he left. I felt relieved: a new woman, whole and strong. A woman who knew her mind. My irritation was gone. I felt happy. There was nothing that upset me again that day. I knew I had relieved myself from a deep-rooted anger that would have found its way out one way or another. I was pleased that it found its right way. I knew he was hurt. But I felt that he needed to confront his own behavior. This was his behavior. To dominate over other people. To go too far. That was not my business. That was his business. But sometimes a big needle is needed to stick into a large pimple.

A few days later he came again, entering quietly. Insecurely. Yet, he came. Took a seat in the same chair. I made some coffee. He was sitting in his chair. I was standing. Stood up for myself. He started saying something, but no words came. His tongue denied him. Then, something cracked inside him and he buried his face in his hands. Then he started to shake. He cried. In the same chair sat the same man. In the same place and yet not. Everything had changed and now was new. I kept standing at the kitchen counter, watching him cry, our family friend. He was sitting in my kitchen, crying. I just stood there, and while witnessing this I slowly and deliberately crossed my arms. Shut myself off. I didn't take responsibility for this. It was as if there were a tiny imp inside me who enjoyed peeking out of my eyes, watching. I let him be, allowed him to peek. Gave him permission. Didn't try to influence him. In some incomprehensible way, I enjoyed having this little rascal within me, laughing inside my head. He filled me with a strange feeling that was somehow pleasing, these lingering moments. I couldn't picture myself walking to the crying man, embracing him and holding him to my heart, comforting him. That was not an alternative. Unconsciously, I somehow realized that if I would now take on the role of the mother, the comforter, there too I would consent to step into his story. That's why I stood with my arms crossed and stuck to my own story. I sensed, as an observer, that each and every one takes responsibility for herself. No one can take responsibility for others. Each person is here on his or her own. Traveling alone. I stuck to my story. I tried to hide the smile that I found was forming on my lips, felt like that would be going too far.

I want to stress that we reconciled fully and that our friendship withstood this incident.

I DON'T REMEMBER at what point exactly I emptied the closets, but it wasn't long after Árni´s death. Somehow, it soon became oppressive to have all his clothes hanging in there, no one using them. The smell of his body faded fairly quickly from the clothes and they started to smell musty. This meant that the time had passed where I could cry with my nose pressed down into the shirt or sweater that he'd last worn. His smell was gone. Forever. I took all his clothes to the Red Cross. At the time, I felt they should go to strangers. Now I regret, though–as I write this–that I didn't put three of his shirts in a box for his daughters to own now as grown-up women. Something from their father to drape over their shoulders when trouble comes their way.

I TOOK A lot of walks. I needed to exercise. I was in need of solitude. Needed to do something to examine and harness the unbridled energy that flowed inside me. Unrestrained. It was pleasant walking in the woods. To feel protected among the trees. To be loved by trees. To find the affection of Mother Nature under my feet. I sensed how I longed to become one with the earth. I wanted to walk naked in the woods. Once, I hiked up a mountain to a waterfall that I could walk behind and see the world with the waterfall's eyes. There, I took my clothes off and bathed naked in the ice cold water. It felt like receiving cascades of nourishment from the fountain of life. I had never been so closely connected to nature. The great mother of all. But how could she fill up the empty space I now felt? I talked to her. I asked her to help me, to love me, to nourish me and heal me.

The path in the woods became the channel of my life. My walk of life. Mostly it was whole and beautifully covered with yellow wooden chips. There, it was soft and supple under my feet. In some places there were occasional roots of trees protruding from the ground and I had to watch my step so that I wouldn't trip over them. In one place there was a large pool of mud. Wet dirt. No dry chips of wood there. Visible tracks by a tractor. Wounds from the tires. Another part was also muddy. Some rocks there instead of wooden chips. The fine chips weren't sufficient there. Under the surface of the path, there trickled a small stream that grew in size each time it rained and sought its channel to the river below. The path came apart at regular intervals, no matter how much an effort was made to mend it. In some places, the path was steep and narrow. Elsewhere, it lay straight and wide. I felt that the path and I were one and the same. It became my life. I had to walk it. At least once a day, sometimes twice. I listened to the trees saying the words I yearned to hear. *Everything will be all right. Everything will be all right.* They sang the words to me. The words I couldn't ask anyone to say to me. But the words I needed to hear. I let the trees speak the words and imagined them embracing me with comfort and whispering in my ears: *Everything will be all right.*

In between my walks I stayed at home. Weeping. Writing, Laughing. Talking on the phone. Yearning for solitude. Sometimes finding it difficult never to be able to take a break from children. Always being alone with children. Living in a house that held conversations now silent. A house without a man. Spirited political discussions were not heard anymore. Speculations about the economy were in the past. No talk about our finances or amorous glances by the kitchen sink. Now, I stood alone doing the dishes. Alone with everything I wanted to talk about. Here, there were no trees to listen to me. Only the dead walls. But those walls preserved everything that we had had together. They'd listened to every word said in their presence. Speculations about our income, the raising of our children, our future plans, our visions for the future, our longings. They kept this all but couldn't give any comfort. Because they were dead walls, not living trees. I listened a great deal to music. One CD, in particular, that I'd bought after Árni died. The only one I listened to for three months. I played it many times a day. Some other music was played only for the sake of appearance. I was fed on the words in these lyrics:

These days are long
These days are oh so long
Hold me in the middle of the night
Say everything is all right
Your love is strong
Your love is oh so strong
Love me in the middle of the night
Say everything will be all right
(Jóhann Helgason)

WIDOW. It was odd how loathsome this word was to my ears when I had become one myself. I was now a widow, though I did not wish to be one and no matter how hard I tried not to use this word, there are people who use it to refer to me and in the national register I'm listed as a widow. To me this word has the connotation of some witchlike older woman in an old movie, all dressed in black, wearing a long skirt reaching down to her mid-calves, thin legs, ugly low-heeled shoes. She has a distant air around her and wears a black veil covering her face. She is alone and everything around her is cold and grey. For this reason I felt that this word was both cold and black and I was startled when I heard it used about me for the first time. I was in some place with a group of people and we met some other people that I didn't know very well, or they me, and one from my group introduced me as Árni's widow. I was startled, and thought, are they talking about me? Actually, it felt more like I was being spoken of. It was uncomfortable and I felt uncomfortable being the dead man's wife. I was the young woman in the village who lost her husband. I was the young widow. Then, gradually, you adjust to this word like other things in the grieving.

You who were before, where have you gone?
Why don't I relish your nearness?
Where are your eyes that looked into mine before?
Where are your hands that held mine?
Where is your body that became one with mine?

I put my daughters to bed. Read them a story. Wanted to go out and walk to the cemetery. Half an hour walk. They soon fell asleep and I put on my overcoat. The air was bitterly cold. I walked along the main street. Always kept to the common routes. Walked there without thinking. Never went off the beaten track. It wasn't until a friend of mine mentioned this and asked me why I didn't use the walking trails that were all over the village. It just hadn't crossed my mind that I could take another route and walk a different path. I found this an interesting comment. Always on the common route. It was like that tonight. I trod the same paths as I used to. Still, I did want to walk less-traveled roads. But that didn't seem to happen automatically. I walked the route by routine. Maybe it gave me a sense of security in my insecure situation to walk the streets I knew so well. I had a need for being in a safe area. I couldn't keep myself afloat endlessly in the middle of the ocean, desperately seeking a stable rock. I had to walk a path I knew. When I had passed the outskirts of the village, and was heading the way straight to you, the flood came. The tears poured from my eyes into the night. The sounds from my throat cut through the silent air.

The woman walking here seemed to be drunk. She didn't walk straight. I watched her and saw how the tears streamed down her cheeks. She talked with a strange voice. Sometimes it sounded as if she had lost her breath. The words rushed irregularly out of her mouth. She obviously carried a heavy burden. Where was she headed? Now I saw it. Crying, she was on her way to the cemetery. The cemetery was in a public place. She must have lost someone close to her, whom she loved. She walked firmly into the cemetery and straight to one of the graves. There was a cross on the grave. She stopped there. She called something out. Looked to the sky and spoke. Suddenly, she fell silent. Put one of her hands into her coat pocket to get a handkerchief. She dried her eyes and blew her nose. It was as if she calmed down then. Was able to catch her breath. All of a sudden, she raised her voice and started to sing. Not loud, though; it was as if she didn't really want to disturb the silence of the night. As if she wanted the silence to accompany the song. The song was about love and hope. When she finished singing she began to cry again. She bent and lay down on the grave. I heard her say, "*My love, it's so cold here with you.*"

She lay there for a while–until she felt cold herself. Then, she rose, dried her eyes and made the sign of a cross over the grave. She walked firmly out the cemetery and never looked back. She continued to walk briskly towards home. She always kept to the common route.

It was past midnight. She lay in her bed. He wasn't with her and would never be. Would never again share this bed with her. She thought about him. Stretched her hand over to his side of the bed. Where he had slept before. Empty. Cold as ice. She wept. Drew her hand back under the warm duvet. Was empty herself. Breathed unevenly as with a kind of sobbing, like she had pain in her chest. She moved her hands under her nightgown. Touched her breasts. Felt her breasts ache from longing for being touched. Caressed them. Squeezed them. They filled up her palm. Pretended that her hands were his hands. She stepped out of bed and took off all her clothes. Slipped again naked under the warm duvet. Pretended she was about to meet him. Drew the duvet carefully over herself as a protective cover.

I SCRUTINIZED the landscape thoroughly. My mind floated over the landscape and I felt as if I'd undressed the land. Peeked at the skin of the earthen body. Found there was heat and fire. I imagined that nature could love me. Fulfill my need. I wanted to undress and walk naked in nature. Become a part of the landscape and be kissed by the sky. My mind soared over waterfalls and mountains. I looked over small creeks and peered into cracks. I sensed how I wanted to rest naked in the embrace of this great earthen body. Roll in the grass and get scraped on sharp small rocks. To merge completely with the flesh of the earth. Feel his eyes in woods and rocks looking at me. I wanted to lie stark naked on the ground and be loved by it. To roll, to be touched and caressed.

I trusted that everyone but me was still asleep in this community. I woke up long before the newspaper delivery boy. I put on a thin summer dress and shoes and drove to my woods, to the trees I knew, the soft purling sound of the stream, and to my favorite tiny white flower with seven petals reaching out from the core, which grew in the summer. The weather was warm and the sun was about to rise. Drowsiness in the air and the day stretching after the night's sleep. Life swelled inside of me and I began my walk. Took my circle as I usually did. There was no one around but I glanced carefully through the surroundings. Then I took off my dress and stood stark naked, embraced by my friends, the trees. I was filled with nature and have no words to describe it. I was part of nature. I went off the path and took off my shoes. I lay down and rolled on the earth. Gazed up into the sky. Stood barefoot in a soft moss with stretched arms up into the air. I was a human tree, I sucked in energy through the soles of my feet, branches shot out of my head, my eyes, my ears, my neck, my breasts and my shoulder blades, which immediately grew green leaves. Life continues. I get to live. I get to bloom. The earth power floods through me. Fills me. Then I tied my shoes back on, walked and ran, walked and ran. I could feel the warm morning breeze touch my body, my breasts, my privates. And as I ended the circle of my walk I threw the dress over me right before I met this man on his early morning walk. I smiled good morning to him, and wondered what his reaction might have been if he had met me stark naked.

It was an odd experience to see regular obituaries in the newspaper about the people who had been with Árni at the Cancer Ward. Many of them and some I had gotten to know. All now taking the same path. Checking themselves out of this world. On the same path all of us are on but these were further along the road.

Our four-year-old daughter: "Mommy, it is all right to be sad when someone has died."

"Yes, Honey, that's all right."

"Mommy, is it also all right to be glad even if someone has died."

"Yes, my love, that's quite all right."

During the period when I cried the most, I felt I needed a mascara that could withstand my tears and wouldn't run down and mess my cheeks. I was fed up with wiping black streaks from my cheeks and looking into those tearful swollen eyes in the mirror, with pale lashes that needed coloring. I went to the drug store.

"Do you have mascara that is tear resistant?"

"Resistant to what?"

"Tears."

"Yes, well, we do have waterproof mascara. You're probably looking for that."

"Yes, I need mascara that stays despite all the tears that pour from my eyes. I don't know when they will stop flowing."

"That will be 1.484 kronas."

I bought the mascara and used it the next day, but that was a day without tears. But the mascara did turn out to be tear proof and now I could cry as much as I wanted without black streaks. I didn't care if my eyes were red and swollen. That was nobody's business. But I didn't like the black streaks and the colorless eyelashes.

I've liked to take a sip of red wine with a good meal on weekends. Now, the weekends were different; now there was no other person to share a fine meal with a glass of wine and to share time and space to take the conversations to a deeper level. Sometimes I invited a friend for dinner who was recently divorced, and her son, and we sometimes met at her house. Our children played. We had some wine and deep conversations that were helpful. Some evenings when I was alone I felt the grief overwhelming me, I felt the temptation to have a glass of wine. One evening when I felt miserable, I did take a glass. Still, I was aware as I poured the wine that something was "not right" about this. Alone at home, kids sleeping, overcome by grief, drinking wine. As it turned out, it was not a good combination.

NOT SO LONG after the funeral, Jercy started calling me. He had come a long way to Árni's funeral. I did not know him, but he knew Árni a little. When I saw him at the funeral, he caught my attention and I was surprised to see him there. About twenty years my senior. I thought he was showing Árni great respect by attending. Then he started calling. I was surprised at first. Jercy was philosophically minded, educated, had read many books and had had rich life experiences. It was fun talking to him. He worked with people. He started calling on a regular basis and it was obvious what he had in mind. We often had good conversations on the phone. He told me that he wanted to invite me and my daughters to Reykjavík; a change of environment would do us some good, he said. He repeated this on numerous occasions. Once, he said that he'd won some money in a lottery and would like me to have it. I felt resistance and from him I wanted neither an invitation to Reykjavík nor any money. I didn't want me to become obligated to him. We still spoke on the phone, though. In the fall, when I traveled to Reykjavík, I gave in and met him. He invited me for a dinner which I accepted.

He had a car and picked me up. We went to a restaurant that specialized in meat and fish. The meal was good and we had some red wine. The evening was nice but this night I was completely convinced that I did not in any way want to engage in a close relationship with this man. After the meal Jercy wanted to drive me home. He showed no hesitation in driving the car despite having drunk quite a lot of wine. At this moment, the fear for my own life surfaced wildly. I stared at the man with my mouth wide open and asked if he was really going to drive the car. What should I do? I, who had just lost my husband and had three little girls at home who needed me. Was I now to take a seat in a car with a man who'd been drinking alcohol? That was out of the question. Princess Diana had died only few days earlier after having ridden in a car with a drunk driver. I became petrified and told him I would not step into the car with him. No way. I'd call a taxi. In this moment, I was aware that if I did drive with him and if an accident would happen, I would never be able to forgive myself.

Jercy kept on calling me but now in a more distinct way, I made it clear to him that I didn't want anything to do with him. He got angry and our relations ended abruptly. I didn't want to attach myself to him. He felt that he'd shown me generosity and to confirm that he told me that he did give a large sum of money to the memorial fund for Árni. I somehow understood that this unknown man had spotted me, when I was helpless and mournful and in great need of comfort, and that he had meant to comfort me, had meant to fill up the space in me. He was himself in deep need of nearness and touch. I shuddered to think of myself filling the emptiness in some other, as hollow as I was myself. I hadn't said good-bye to the love I had for Árni. It was still alive. But I did very well understand this man. He was at exactly the same spot as I was, in desperate need of love and touch and he imposed these expectations upon me. Hopes that I neither could nor wanted to satisfy. Was I to enter into a relationship with a man only because he wanted me? He fantasized about me in his dreams. He played with me through his imagination. Human frailty. Imperfection of being human. That's how we are, humans. It takes an effort to live; it takes an effort to distinguish between a longing and an obsession. It's a lifelong struggle to be a human being.

I sometimes wondered how people looked at me in my new role. Who this woman was who had recently lost her husband to cancer? To the disease no one wanted to get but hit wherever and whoever at whatever age and no one knew who'd be the next one. The disease all people feared. Cancer. Sign of death. How did this woman cope? How did she survive? And now she was on her own with her three daughters. A dead man's wife.

My daughters' roles also changed. Now, there was no daddy anymore to help them with various concerns from school or elsewhere. Now drawings of the family showed a mommy, all the girls, the cat and then Daddy, an angel with wings. And now, every time a form had to be filled out for them, applying for summer camps and such, it was necessary to mention specifically that their father was deceased. I've always found it difficult to write on the form, Father: Árni Margeirsson, deceased.

Our small business, an advertising agency, had now been running for five years. We had named it *NinetySeven – Advertising Agency*. The name referred to the area code for East Iceland, which was 97 before the age of mobile phones. Árni had been certain that the year 1997 would be the year of good luck for us, the year when our business would start thriving and we did have expectations. But no one can foresee the future. The year 1997 was the year he died, and it was the year when I sold the business, which had started to grow. Just before Árni was diagnosed with cancer, the first employee came in, a young industrial designer who took care of the business along with another employee who was hired during Árni's hospitalization. He was a graphic design student. They managed the agency while Árni lay ill and after he died. I faced a crucial question afterward, whether I wanted to continue managing the business on my own. In a small community every business makes a difference and this advertising agency served all of East Iceland. Members of the Economic Committee of Egilsstadir encouraged me to continue the operation of the agency. They said it would be in the interest of the business, and also of the community if I did so. I felt they did acknowledge our efforts, but I also asked myself what would be in my own interest. My life was such right now that I was unable to make a crucial decision. I was aware of that, and knew that the agency was a dream of his, not mine.

I thought a lot about reasons regarding our business, whether to sell it or not and the benefits either way. The thought of having to manage a profitable business in order to sufficiently run my home was overwhelming. I knew that wasn't what I wanted. I thought and I thought. I came to see that I could either make a decision based on benefits for the business, in the belief it was in the best interest of the agency that I continue to run it. But I wasn't sure this was true. I could make my decision with focus on the benefits for the community, and decide to run the business so it would continue its operation in the village. Or I could make my decision based on my own interests, put the business up for sale and withdraw from its operation.

That was the decision I made, and I knew it was the right one for me. I sold the business without any feeling of guilt; I did not feel that I was betraying Árni. The business had been a dream of his and now he wasn't here anymore to live the dream. I felt lucky to have realized so soon that you cannot live another person's dream. Not even your spouse's. You are hardly able to cope with making your own dreams come true. This was an opportunity for me to think about dreams. At this point, I decided I would look at Árni's death as an opportunity for me to make changes and to examine my own dreams. To do something with my own life.

As the first winter was passing by, I started to feel anxiety over the coming Christmas. I couldn't bear the thought of celebrating it at home. It was somehow an overwhelming thought. I decided to take my daughters to the Canary Islands. It was good to escape the darkness and get into the sun and the warm climate. We spent three weeks there. Every day was similar to the others except for Christmas Eve, when we exchanged gifts, like at home. We were constantly reminded that we were missing one from our family because there were families everywhere around us enjoying their time together. But it wouldn't have mattered where we'd been over Christmas time, this gap was a fact and we had to live with it. In fact, I don't remember this Christmas clearly, I was overcome with sorrow, alone with my girls all the time, and saw nothing but families in their togetherness, where all of them were alive and enjoying life. This Christmas is somewhere in my amnesia. When the next one approached, I did look forward to celebrating it with my girls. We enjoyed the holidays, though they were no more memorable than other Christmases, but I was so relieved for not having to go elsewhere. On New Year's Eve we visited Árni's grave in the cemetery and we all lighted torches over it, giggling with joy with him and about him, celebrating the New Year, all happy to be together at home.

A FEW DAYS after Árni died the doorbell rang. A man was standing on the doorstep holding an envelope. He handed it to me,–it was full of money—and said that this was an indication of gratitude from him and his wife towards Árni and me for all the good things we had contributed to this small community. He told me that he had wished to bring me a little something as a sign of how thankful our community was for our participation in social affairs, and the way we'd worked for the greater good of this small society. This man was an entrepreneur in Egilsstadir who had been taken ill and been admitted to the hospital around the same time as Árni lay on his deathbed in the Cancer Ward. He'd paid Árni a visit, even though they hardly knew each other. I remember clearly how glad Árni was that this man would take the time to come and see him. And now he stood on my doorstep, deeply moved, and passed me the envelope. And that was all he said.

I received another small envelope in the mail shortly after Árni died. In it there was a receipt for a deposit of 15.000 kronas to my account. The transfer was made to a branch of a bank in the west part of Reykjavík. The name of the depositor wasn't filled out. I didn't know many people who lived in the west part of Reykjavík. I thought, how wonderful some people are. I had thoughts of gratitude towards this person.

A month later another envelope came and I called the branch to ask about the transfer. The woman in the bank told me that she could not trace it since it was done anonymously. I told her about my situation and this deposit to my account from someone unknown to me who obviously intended to support me. She then told me that she knew of an elderly man who regularly came to the bank for the errands of putting money into the accounts of people he didn't know but wanted to support. She was unable to tell me more.

The third month, yet another receipt arrived, and on it was typed in small letters that I would not receive any more receipts but I should keep checking my account. For a year and a half, I received payments from this anonymous elder man who namelessly made this act of charity by supporting me and my daughters. I pictured him as an old man wearing an overcoat, entering the bank every month, depositing this money into my account. I visualized him as having read the obituary about my husband and making a decision to support his family. I was moved by my anonymous benefactor and his method of showing support. He didn't need to be recognized for his good deeds. He made them in silence. I take the opportunity here to thank this kind hearted man for his support of me and my daughters.

It's distressing having to stand in front of a counter in some office in order to have your deceased spouse's accounts closed or to have transactions stopped because your spouse has died. It's almost unbearable to need to say out loud that he's dead. The thought of having to do this is hard, but it is worse having to stand there, and to wait in a line to be the next one up to the counter, to notify the person behind the counter of the death of your spouse. It's so difficult to say it out loud because you're still trying to figure it out yourself.

A year after Árni died, I got a call from a publishing company selling books. I wasn't interested. At the end of the call, the woman on the other end asked me if my number was also registered to someone else. This was a sensitive issue. It took a year for a name to be removed from the printed telephone directory. At that time there was no Internet-based directory. I told the woman that it was not up to me to tell her whose telephone number this was and we had a brief argument over the phone. I did not want to tell her of the possibility that the number might also still be listed in Árni's name. I did not want to have any discussions with a complete stranger about the recent death of my husband, who had called me to sell me books. This annoyed me. I don't recall how our conversation ended, if I told her that no one else was listed under this number or whether I continued saying that I needn't to inform her about it. Two hours later the same woman called again and asked for Árni. I got angry and asked her when the list of names she was using had been compiled; it was from the previous year. I told her that I found it unacceptable that she'd do the work from an old list of names, and expect prospective customers to update it for her. The publishing company should provide her with a new list. Thus ended the conversation.

Two days later she calls yet again and asks for Árni. At that point, I got furious with the poor woman and told her that I would write to the manager of the company and inform him of the distress it may cause when using old lists of names. I wrote a sharp letter to him and received in turn a letter of apology and a box full of various books on offer as a compensation for the mistake.

❁

I HAD VARIOUS reasons to get angry and blame others during the process of Árni's illness. For one, I was unable to establish contact with his oncologist when we came to Reykjavík. In Akureyri, I had been used to being able to call Árni's doctor anytime or to stop him in the corridor, asking about his condition. That was a big change for me as a family member not being able to talk to the doctor when I met him in the corridor in the hospital in Reykjavík. Each passing day, Árni became more and more ill, and I could feel his health ebbing away. This caused me anguish and I was angry with the doctor. But I was able to call our doctor in Akureyri who in turn called the doctor in Landspitali in Reykjavík for me to ask about Árni's condition. He phoned me back to inform me of the latest status. I once called our doctor in Akureyri Hospital from the Cancer Ward where I was looking directly at the oncologist while I asked the other doctor to contact him to bring me the latest new on Árni's condition. My contact or rather lack of contact with the oncologist could certainly have caused me to feel stuck in my anger.

A year after Árni died, I met a woman who had then recently lost her husband. We started talking about our common experience and she told me the course of her husband's illness that he had undergone a liver biopsy and therefore was not supposed to move for twenty-four hours. I asked her why that was, because Árni had needed to be pricked with a needle through his liver to reach his gallbladder but we hadn't got any information about his having to stay put. I was totally unaware of this. The woman told me that there is a risk of internal bleeding. At hearing this, a story took form inside of my head. This evening when the needle was pricked into his liver, Árni walked down the ward corridor to refresh himself. The bleeding had started the following night.

It continued and increased, which resulted in blood transfusion and an operation, which then led to palliative treatment, with him ending up on the respirator and finally dying a week later. The story in my head disturbed me and I wondered why nobody remembered to tell us that he should have kept resting for twenty-four hours. That was probably why what happened happened. At this point, I could easily have allowed my anger to push me ahead into searching medical journals and blowing this up into a case. But I understood that it wouldn't have made any difference. Árni may have lived a little longer, suffered more, in another way, but he would have died. But I could have allowed this anger to grow as a seed in my mind. I chose to not let that happen.

THREE OR FOUR years after Árni's death, I went to the mall to look at some shoes. In the shoe store I saw a young father with his two young daughters who were trying on their shoes for Christmas. Witnessing them, it all poured over me. I hurried out of the store, practically ran out of the mall and into my car, where I allowed my tears to flow.

And ten whole years after his death, on an inland flight, a couple with three daughters sat down next to me. Two of the girls were quite young and one a bit older. They were at similar ages as our daughters were when Árni died. I was reminded. I allowed myself to escape into a corner inside of myself and weep a little, but then I felt glad looking at them and thought about how lucky they were to be together with all those girls, and hoped they would receive the gift from life to be together until the girls grew up to be adults.

My daughters felt the loss of their father. Children come home with assignments from school to ask Mom or Dad for help with them. But this is also the case with children whose parents have divorced or don't live with their parents. Dad or Mom isn't always there for their children.

Music also reminded us of the loss. During Árni's last days in the Intensive Care, we'd played the pan flute. For a long time, tears came without warning if I heard such music.

With Árni being dead, it was easier to remember the good moments from our life and to talk about them. It became easy to praise him to the skies as a person and to make him almost a saint. I may have done that. It may be that we who go on living have a tendency to do just that.

I felt, when Árni died, that a human life wasn't really to be measured in the number of years lived, that, in fact, it doesn't all matter how long each person gets. There were other principles of worth, principles that I don't understand but have some inner belief in. Maybe it was my attempt to feel relief. The human mind tends to assert that it is better to live a good life for a short while than a bad life for a long time. The human mind also tends to believe that there is a purpose to all this. What is this purpose? Is there a purpose? Is it maybe concealed from us? Is it important for a man to know his own purpose? Does man only live in service for the Universe and the circulation of life. Does it matter what we do with our lives? Are we allowed to use life at our own discretion? Do we have the freedom to choose? Or are we strategically placed in order to take on particular assignments? Assignments that do not necessarily seem to benefit ourselves?

I gained a new understanding of the saying "take care in the presence of a soul."

I had suddenly myself become the sensitive soul spoken of, so susceptible at certain moments on my path of pain and uncertainty. At that time, I suddenly recognized the meaning of the act of being cautious, being considerate in relations with people. And I also came to discover that I hadn't so much put any particular efforts into showing caution with other people. I also discovered that with certain events in your life, a turning point occurs in your comprehension of life itself, when suddenly you realize what was knowledge before now becomes understanding.

After Árni's death, the question sometimes came to my mind, how would I react if one of my children died. I had a strong feeling that no one who is born into this world has a guarantee certificate to walk the path of life without trauma. There will be shocks, no matter what, although no one wants to experience them.

Do you remember when you kissed me under lampposts on our way home from a dance? This was long before you got ill. We were walking home after having had great a fun. We'd danced a lot and long into the night. Then you stopped under a lamppost as we walked, holding hands on our way home, and you said, "I really like kissing you under a lamppost." You drew me into the beam, held me tight, and kissed me a long kiss. Your kiss was cold because it was frosty outside and a drop from your nose touched my cheek. Still, the kiss was warm. There were ten or twelve lampposts on our way home.

"Mmm …," you said and led me under the next post. Hereafter, this was repeated after dances. It was different in the summer because then the nights were bright. They were more enchanting and your kisses warmer. The posts were put to good use and we used them all, even though there was no light beam. The beam was much greater; it was the bright summer night.

It made me extroverted. This strong energy. Gave me a new feeling for myself, a special sense of my own body. My awareness moved from one part to another. Often, located between my legs; then it moved up to my breasts, that longed for touch. I was a woman, felt I was a goddess. No one knew of my thoughts or how I felt. No one sensed my longing. It was strong. My need uncontrollable. I became unrestrained, felt hollow on the inside. Like all that was before had been scraped out from my insides. Desired to be filled again, filled with the juice of life. Yearned for caressing hands on me, a hot naked body next to mine, a breath in my ear, a look into desiring eyes. Was myself extreme and irrational. Felt tempted by the sight of naked male flesh in the swimming pool. Wanted to attack it, swallow it for my own satisfaction. I was empty.

Or else, I would feel deep aversion, detesting flesh, couldn't bear the nature of being human. But it depended on to whom the flesh belonged. Some of the flesh I couldn't stand. Mainly on those who wanted to approach me. Some sought my presence. They had empathy for me, felt sorry for me. But they experienced as well and maybe more deeply pain in their own inadequacy. I think they had a longing to fill me. Saw my hollowness and wanted to absorb me. Fill me with their own needy hunger. And there was flesh out there that I desired. How could I survive this? What had happened? My husband was dead and left me hollow. Who should now fill me? What was to become of me? How could I control my unrestrained urges that regularly kept on showing themselves? They always emerged at a certain time. Always at the same point in my menstrual period. Where was my mind? Why did this unbridled desire that appeared like a wild beast seem to be located down there only? Was it merely biological? Was this grief? No one had mentioned that those feelings were part of bereavement. That grief would even entail desiring one's friends and comforters and that I would become a plaything of my own emotions and urges, and have no one to confide in about this. To play imaginary games with people by sending them thoughts and fantasizing about acts that could never ever take place in reality. I tried to tame the frenzied mind of mine that spurred my instincts, which I had no control over. Now, I felt that I could, to some extent, grasp the existence and anguished minds of those who force others into sexual relations of some sort. They're not acting on their own volition. Emptiness and agony are their life companions. These companions now stood at my door offering their company. My greatest fear was that I would accept their offer. I feared that I would end up lost on my way, become a victim of my uncontrollable urges.

Your beauty may to some extent have stemmed from being aware that your death was approaching. Those who know they're about to die begin to live life in a different way. It's as if they live in a different awareness, as if life appears to them in another way.

My youngest daughter asked me one day, "Mommy, can you die too?"

How are we supposed to answer a small child who asks such a question? She was five or six. I felt I couldn't just say to her, "No, no, of course no, I can't die."

Because I was thinking exactly the same thing and I had never been as conscious of my own mortality as now, after Árni's death. I reflected on her question and felt that I could by no means promise her that I would live. I gave her the answer that at some point we would all die, such was life, but now there weren't any signs of me dying and we would have to trust that I would continue to live. I don't know if I did answer her in a right way. There is no right answer to this question. Yet, I felt that I wasn't able to promise her that I would not die because I don't know how many days of life I will get.

Being the one parent left, I started to be more aware of my own mortality. I found myself thinking of accidents and death. Such could happen anytime. I had learned that you can't take anything for granted, and that this life is only lent to us, we have no guarantees, not even for living this day to its end. Often, as I stood on my doorstep, inserted the key in the door lock in order to lock it, lifted the door handle and turned the key, I found out how mortal I was. For some reasons I felt it most when I turned the key. Maybe a thought occurred somewhere back in my mind that it could possibly be my last turning the key. I was on my way to work, into the traffic, and I thought, "Today I could die." I felt I was valuable, and I began thinking of the influence I have on the lives of others. If I were to die, three girls would be orphaned, and other people would raise them. That would have a great effect on my daughters and change the lives of others too. I did not want to think about this, but it remained in my head. Suddenly, it was as if I acquired a deeper sense of life as a whole, saw it somehow in a new way and with a greater perspective, and at the same time I became more aware of how influential we are, as humans; everything we do and say has an influence and that is important.

The more I contemplated this, the better I understood that it wasn't enough for me to just be alive for my little girls. I wanted all the best for them. I wished that their lives would be free of pain, there was enough pain already. I felt it stronger than ever that I was the glue in their life. I suddenly realized how the parental role is almost omnipotent. I grasped that what I did for myself, I also did for them. I saw that in order to take care of my girls I had to take care of myself first. I was their role model and my biggest gift to them was to participate in life myself, to show them that I was taking responsibility for myself as a human being and making an effort to achieve some goal in my life. Gradually, I decided to regard Árni's death as a chance for me to make changes and venture into something new. I took two lucky steps. A year after he died, I studied yoga teacher training at Kripalu Center in the US and a year later I enrolled in a distance-learning program, writing and literature, at Vermont College of Norwich University, also in the US, where I earned my BA. That changed my life and I started to envision myself as a writer. I made some changes in my life and tried to focus more and more on writing along with every day duties and businesses.

One of my good friends talked to me shortly after the funeral; she wanted to make a book or an album for us as a memorial for Árni. She made the book in a personal way with a painting made by Árni that she glued to the front page. This book became a great treasure for us. We collected the obituaries on him, old clippings from old newspapers with drawings that Árni had sent in as a kid. I found his identity card from when he was a young man, and an old passport and two old driver's licenses that I glued into the book. Also some pictures from our daily life, several drawings and cards our daughters had made, and pictures from his funeral. Árni wrote some poetry during the time he was ill and we also found a place in the book for that. I wrote some poems and reflections on love and life that I put in as well. The book is a treasure of memories in words and pictures.

Our neighbors, a couple living on the same street, got divorced around the time Árni died. They had three children. Their financial situation was bad and the husband had a problem with alcohol, which was one of the reasons for their divorce. They got little sympathy from our community. At the same time as my neighbors and the people in our small community came to me and brought me gifts, flowers, food and money, comfort, support and friendship, very few came to visit my neighbor to support her. No one had died in her home, but her husband, the breadwinner, had left, and her home was just like mine, a bleeding wound. I sympathized with her. I thought she was really as alone as I was. On her own, carrying solely all the responsibility, alone with her children. Alone, with broken dreams.

WOMEN HAVE said to me that there is probably nothing as damaging as to be abandoned by your husband for another woman. It is so painful to be betrayed. They think it's even a little bit better to lose a husband to death than into the arms of another woman, when an enormous anger and rejection will follow. Besides, the corpse is alive, and, often, there's no way to avoid running into it now and then.

I received many beautiful memorial gifts when Árni died. Crosses, angels, porcelain candle holders with engraved words of comfort and condolence. I cared for these gifts and often lit the candles and placed the crosses and engraved prayers in prominent places. It was a part of my daily life to light a candle for Árni. As time passed, I hadn't as much need to do it. Then one day, when I looked over my living room, I suddenly felt overwhelmed to see so many crosses and angels that reminded me of grief and death. Suddenly, I couldn't bear this and from then on, if someone gave me a gift related to bereavement or death, it irritated me. Two years or so passed until I started to feel like this. I may not have realized it at once but, in fact, this was a good sign; I was moving away from my grief. This was a sign that I was finding a new direction, becoming ready to live life again on my own and in new terms, not in the shadow of sorrow. I put these things away. I couldn't bear to think of myself spending the days lighting all these candles and having those memorial crosses in front of my eyes. I didn't want to be in this same position four years after Árni's death, still mourning him so much. I took these objects and packed them, and next time I tidied up, I gave them away. Life wasn't anymore to revolve only around lighting a candle for my beloved Árni each day, no matter how much I loved him. Our life together was over and now it was mine to turn to other tasks but hold on to him, a dead man. I would have to let go of him. Now, I light a candle in his name on days of celebration, on special days in the lives of my daughters and also when I am facing a difficult decision. In such moments, I light a candle for Árni.

I began to feel an increasing discomfort living in our small society, two years after Árni died. My role had changed, in every way. Both inwardly and outwardly, towards other people. We lived in a good community with plenty of space for everyone. But now, I did not find a space for me there any longer. I had three female friends who all divorced about the same time as Árni died and we met occasionally and had a good time together. But now I sensed in a new way how communities are tailored to couples.

I didn't find a place there anymore. In small communities, people know too much about each other and single women take notice when a single man moves to the village. They start to get excited and the point is who will be the first one to catch him. I wanted to move to a larger community with more people and more options for both my daughters and myself.

We moved to Gardabaer in the capital area three years after Árni's death. It was my old hometown. The village was now much bigger than it was when I used to live there. I was able to buy an apartment with three bedrooms. Our youngest two made friends with girls in the neighborhood on the first day. The schools for all of them were at a short distance from our new home. They were good schools and the girls were doing well. Addy went for six months as an exchange student to Boulder, Colorado.

But the years go by, children become adults and life changes. That is one thing that is certain – life will change. After my daughters left the nest, I bought a small apartment in central of Reykjavik. Through the years I have had all kinds of jobs but now I focus on teaching yoga and writing. I have concentrated on to put life struggle aside and been more focused on the idea that "less is more." I feel comfortable with that and live a simple life. I hike every day and swim in the cold sea of Iceland. I have not remarried but been in short relationships. I really would like to find a life companion.

I WORE MY wedding ring for a few months after Árni died, sometimes on my finger, sometimes around my neck, with his ring. Then I laid my ring inside of his in my jewelry box. When my oldest daughter moved away from home and went abroad for her studies I gave her her father's ring. And several years later, when I started working with a group of people who had lost their spouses, we had a discussion on what could be done with the wedding ring. After that discussion I got the idea to have both of the rings melted together and cast into three sister rings. My daughters thought this was a brilliant idea and arranged for them to be made. Now they all carry their parents' wedding rings in a transformed mold.

At the time of this writing, two of our daughters live in Denmark and study at the University of Copenhagen. Addy is studying medicine and Erla Maria is taking biology to prepare herself for dentistry. Una lives in Iceland and works in a nursing home. They are all wonderful persons and I am grateful to have had the lifetask of being their mother.

It's good to be able to look back and see that we could go through this time together, through this then-new future that scared me and made me feel vulnerable. Looking back, I see things that I wish I had done differently but things done then will never be changed. At that time, my only wish was to be able to live long enough so I could be present for our daughters till they were grown-up women. That has come true. Life goes on and this year, I will be a grandmother ...

In my survival, what often helped me to be fully present was to meditate, write, take walks and practice yoga. All these methods gave me opportunities to step out of the mundane everyday life, out of my mourning, or sometimes to more consciously enter it, gave me a time and space for myself and my reflections, and allowed me to be in my body. My grief was deep; it was not just subjective or emotional. It lay on my chest like a heavy rock and beneath this rock was the hollowness, the void that had no way to be filled. Therefore, it was good to calm the mind, follow the breathing while meditating, breathe deeply and connect more deeply to the body through yoga postures, find the soles of my feet, step rhythmically on the ground during my walks and sit down writing when everyone was asleep, transforming my tears to words.

The walks filled me with vigor that gave me the strength to continue. I went to my little woods where I could make my half-hour circle. I often walked two circles. Once, as I stood at the edge of the woods looking over the town, I received a confirmation somehow; I just "knew" that I had to accept all of my feelings, whatever they might be, the bad ones, too. Allow them all to come, but not necessarily act on them. Not judge them. Just say to myself, "Yes, this is how it is now," without scolding myself for having bad feelings. I realized how deep grief is and how it takes its toll. It plays on every string of the emotional scale and in order for us to heal and become whole again we must also listen to the somber strings of sorrow. That's how we create the symphony we need to be able to carry on.

Meditation gave me the chance to soothe myself, follow my breathing, listen to the surrounding sounds, and discern how I felt in this moment. It gave me space, for a few moments, to set the grief aside and observe how I breathed and how I lived in the present. There are various meditation techniques. I meditated once a week with my female friends, we said prayers and took turns in leading the way into all kinds of spiritual journeys that also served as a valuable period of rest from the daily hassle.

Practicing yoga gave me inner peace. Going to a yoga class in the afternoon, withdrawing from the everyday pressures, noticing the breathing and the movements of the body, connecting movement and breathing, holding yoga postures and keeping attention and focus on breathing and body gave me some splendid freedom and space that was full of peace. At the end of the yoga classes there was a fifteen- minute relaxation period and that was the height of the class for me. My body would relax after exercising and let go. In one such class, I had a profound experience. I thought that Árni came to me. He was happy and we greeted and embraced each other, thanking each other for the time we'd had together. He said to me that our paths had diverged. We were meant to go in opposite directions. My eyes brimmed with tears; I lay on the floor crying. It was a beautiful experience and I felt how it filled me with gratitude and a kind of acceptance. I practiced yoga twice a week and after each class, I had a feeling of ease, a sense of freedom, a feeling of inner happiness and peace. I felt it mostly in the patience I had towards my daughters when I came home from the yoga class. That was the gift from my yoga practice. Then everything felt *all right*.

Writing gave me comfort, too. I have always had an urge to write but I had put it aside when the everyday chores of life called for my attention, along with the raising of my daughters. But in the bereavement, I sat down and wrote and wrote. Put my circumstances and experiences on paper and cried myself through my writings. I wrote crying, both on my computer and in my diaries. Wrote poetry. Found relief in putting my words on paper. The blank sheet became my confidant. But it wasn't easy to write about all this. At first, I felt a sense of guilt when I expressed some of my thoughts, doubted I had the courage to put my thoughts into words. Interestingly, though, after my thoughts were on paper, no matter how difficult the process was, they didn't burden me as before. For me, this is the power of writing.

As I was bringing my story to an end for this book, I picked a book from my bookshelf that I hadn't looked at for a long time. It was Eleven minutes by the Brazilian writer Paul Coelho. Suddenly, I wanted to see what Coelho had written to me in my book when he visited Iceland many years ago. I opened it and read his handwritten words, "Anna, pay the price of your dreams!" I had waited for an hour in a line to meet him and when it was my turn, I sat in a chair at the table in front of him, put my hand in his, looked into his eyes, and entrusted him with a secret. As I reflected upon this memory, I found that I wished to have a quote from Coelho in my own book. I decided to send him a message through Facebook. I told him about my book and mentioned our handshake. I said that I wanted to ask him for a quotation to put in my book. The next day he wrote the following on his Facebook time line:

> *"When we least expect it, life sets us a challenge to test our courage and willingness to change; at such a moment, there is no point in pretending that nothing had happened or in saying that we are not ready. The challenge will not wait. Life does not look back. A week is more than enough time for us to decide whether or not to accept our destiny."*
>
> *(Paul Coelho, 9 July 2012)*

I SEE ÁRNI come walking down the sidewalk. There he is in his brown and worn fur jacket, with his black Russian fur cap on his head. I know this sight so well. But it's not him. It's been years since he died. This is another man.

§§

VII. ASSIGNMENTS

WHAT CAN I DO?

This chapter contains meditations and assignments that are intended to help you face your new circumstances, calm your mind, and develop self-compassion. The meditations train you in being here and now and can help you from the very beginning to find peace and a better emotional space.

The exercises are made for you, who have lost a spouse and want to help yourself find your way forward in the grieving process and try to understand your newly changed situation. Some of the assignments look back at the past, others to the future.

Before you complete the assignments, it is worth revisiting the chapter on self-compassion. Remind yourself before you start the assignments that you have not chosen to be in this position and it is not your fault. Complete the assignments when you have peace and quiet and will not be disturbed.

You don't have to do the assignments in any particular order. You can work on them one at a time and take the others when you have the opportunity. Work on them in the order that suits you and when you yourself are ready.

The assignments can be a good source of support in the grieving process, but many will find that they need to seek further professional support.

MEDITATION

There are many definitions of meditation. One way of looking at it is that meditation is a way of withdrawing from the chaotic thoughts of daily life, which constantly assail the mind and can keep it completely occupied. When you meditate, you calm your mind by paying attention to the present moment as it is. The most efficient way of calming your mind is to pay attention to your breathing and observe it without thinking about it. Teacher and theosophist Sigvaldi Hjálmarsson said of meditation: "To live the moment sincerely means that everything that approaches the senses and arises in one's mind is accepted unconditionally..." *(A Kind of Silence)*

During meditation, the practitioner reflects on what it is to sense: to see, to hear, to touch. He becomes completely conscious of what he senses. During meditation, stillness descends upon both mind and body. The practitioner dwells in the moment for a while; he is here and now. In such a state, he is more receptive to his own efforts to influence his thoughts and can visualize internally what he wants to happen in his life.

The following are meditations that are intended to help and support you in the wake of your loss.

The first is a short meditation that anyone can try. It is intended to quiet the mind, deepen and slow your breathing and give a feeling of wellness. It's a good starting point.

The gratitude meditation is based on imagination that you engage in after your body has entered a relaxed state. This exercise is made especially for you who have lost a spouse and should help you separate yourself from your deceased spouse.

Before you meditate, make sure you have peace and quiet and won't be disturbed. The practice of these meditation exercises will not give you lasting peace, but doing them from time to time throughout your period of grief can alleviate some of your suffering day by day, which can make them a valuable support in the grieving process in the long term.

Get someone to read the meditations aloud to you.

MEDITATION/RELAXATION

Take a seat on a chair with the soles of your feet on the ground and your spine straight. Close your eyes. Slowly press your shoulders down, stretch the crown of your head upward and lengthen your neck, pointing your chin slightly down toward your chest. This way, your head is in line with your spine and your neck isn't bent. Lay your hands on your thighs, palms facing up or down, whichever you find more comfortable. Move your jaw slowly and make sure it's loose and relaxed. Your tongue is relaxed. Now notice how you are sitting, with your spine straight, your body relaxed, and your feet on the floor. Feel how your body touches the chair, how the soles of your feet touch the floor, and how your hands touch your thighs. As you meditate, your spine may sink backward and your head forward, so take care to remind yourself from time to time to stretch your neck up to the crown of your head, so you're always sitting with your spine straight.

Now take a deep breath through your nose and hold it in for a few seconds. Then exhale slowly through your mouth. Do this three times. Feel how your body relaxes with every exhalation.

Now breathe normally through your nose. Breathe deep into your belly and imagine you are inhaling peace and calm. When you exhale, imagine you are releasing your worries. Again you inhale peace and calm and exhale your anxious thoughts. Once more. Breathe in peace and breathe out everything that troubles you in daily life. Then let go of your breathing and feel how free it is.

Shift your attention to your nose and feel how the air you breathe in and out touches the inside of your nostrils. Focus on this for a while. Feel that the inhalation is cooler and the exhalation warmer. Your body is relaxed now and your mind at peace.

Now you return slowly by first moving your fingers and toes. Then deepen your breathing and open your eyes.

MEDITATION/IMAGINATION – A GRATEFUL MOMENT WITH YOUR BELOVED

This meditation is conceived as a grateful moment with your loved one, imagined and created by you – a moment of thanks for you and your beloved. If your body tenses up at this prospect, take a few deep breaths; inhale peace and calm and exhale your tension. Keep your eyes closed. Make sure your spine is quite straight. Feel yourself to be calm and prepared to imagine this meeting.

Now imagine you see your loved one approach you from a distance, slowly coming closer. Your beloved is close now and you can see his face clearly. Your loved one smiles and comes to you in deep joy. You can feel the love and attraction that drew you to your spouse in the first place and lived with you throughout your relationship.

Your beloved has reached you, and you gaze deep into each other's eyes. If you cry or find this overwhelming, that's alright. Allow yourself to cry, allow yourself to be overwhelmed for a moment.

Come back to the imagined moment again. Your loved one stands before you and you are very close. You now allow your loved one to say something beautiful to you. Remember that this is your imagination and you create the words. Receive these words. Now you say something beautiful to your beloved in return.

Remember that this is a moment of gratitude. Find what you can express thanks for. Allow your loved one to thank you in return. Allow your loved one to encourage you and tell you how he hopes you will live your life now. Allow yourself to cry if you must. Listen to your beloved's words. Receive these words and preserve them in your mind and heart. Perhaps you don't want to reply. But if you find an answer, you can tell your loved one how you wish to respond to the words. Perhaps you want to say this aloud. It can give you strength to hear your own voice express how you want to respond to this encouragement. Allow yourself to cry. Allow yourself to feel pain. Feel what a delicate moment this is. Allow it to be delicate. Feel how tender and precious it is.

Now allow your loved one to embrace you. Allow yourself to be thankful, and allow yourself to take joy in the creation of this beautiful moment with your beloved. Allow the both of you to thank each other in a warm embrace and kiss. Then you bid goodbye and slowly break the embrace. Now you both know that you are not meant to tread the paths of life together any longer.

Though you want to hold on to this moment and your beloved, let go. Your loved one grows more distant, moving further and further away. You can wave to each other if you wish. Allow yourself to cry if you need to.

Your loved one is now gone. Observe how you feel. Bring your attention to your nose and feel the breath touch your nostrils. Now notice how you are seated in your chair. Feel the straightness of the spine and the soles of your feet on the floor.

Take a deep breath now, inhaling peace and calm and exhaling gratitude that spreads throughout the body. Do this three times. Fill yourself with peace and calm, and fill your body with gratitude. Then slowly begin to move your fingers and toes, and open your eyes. Allow yourself to cry some more if you need. You can repeat this exercise later if you want, and it will gradually become easier.

MANTRAS

Mantras are short sentences, or even single words, that are chanted repeatedly, aloud or in your mind. Chanting a mantra is one way to calm and steady your mind. Most known mantras are in Sanskrit, and each mantra has a particular meaning. Their meaning is positive and the mantra is chanted again and again. You can also use meaningless words for the same purpose, repeating them over and over again in your mind to keep distracting thoughts at bay. While the mantra is chanted or repeated in your mind, no thoughts can penetrate.

You can create your own personal mantra, give it a melody, or hum it in your mind. The mantra is chanted repeatedly in your mind or aloud in order to prevent chaotic thoughts or feelings of anxiety.

TRAUMA

The following questions have to do with traumatic experiences. If you have had other traumatic experiences that you didn't process, it is likely that they will affect how you deal with this present trauma.

- Have you had traumatic experiences before?
- What were they?
- Have you processed those experiences?
- What helped you to do so?
- What do you think would help you now?

WHO AM I?

This exercise offers you the opportunity to revisit what you were like before you met your spouse, how you functioned together as a couple, and who you are now.

- Who was I before we met?
- What was my impression of my spouse when we met?
- What were we like as a couple?
- Who am I now?

MY SPOUSE

This assignment can bring forth tears and longing. Feel how good it is to allow yourself to cry and reminisce.

What is the first thing that comes to mind when you think of your spouse?

Describe your husband's/your wife's...

- ... looks, movements, mannerisms, gaze, smell
- ... character
- ... personal qualities
- ... reactions
- ... strengths
- ... weaknesses

Which memory of your spouse gives you strength at this moment?

A LETTER TO YOUR PARTNER

In this assignment, you can write a letter to your husband/wife. Here you will try to put into words what you want to say to your late spouse. Express yourself about anything, whether positive or negative – also things that were difficult. If you want to write about something that was unresolved between you and find you struggle to put it into words, give yourself plenty of time to choose them. You can always edit and correct yourself later in whatever way you want. This allows you the opportunity to put your feelings into words and see things in a different light. The following questions can be points of departure for you to ask yourself even more questions.

- When you think of your spouse, what's the first thing that comes to mind?
- Do you want to tell him or her something in particular? Describe.
- Write something about the good sides of the relationship?
- Write about what was difficult in the relationship?
- Do you feel angry when you think of your husband/wife? Describe.
- Say something kind and loving to him or her?
- What do you want to thank your spouse for?

A LETTER TO YOURSELF

Write yourself a letter. It is unusual to write a letter to yourself, but it is worth the try. Many questions may arise in your mind as you write yourself a letter. Below are some questions to get you started and help you along, so one question can lead to another. Allow your mind to flow. You can also write yourself a letter and skip the questions entirely.

- What are my strengths at the moment?
- What are my weaknesses at the moment?
- For what do I deserve my own gratitude in my relationship with my spouse?
- Is there something weighing on my mind?
- Was there something we had planned to do together that we never did?
- Was there something we didn't do that I want to do now?
- What words of encouragement can I say to myself?

SELF-COMPASSION

This assignment is intended to help you bring out your self-compassion. Give yourself plenty of time to consider and find realistic ways for you to show yourself compassion. Mention a few ways in which you are prepared to take action. It's most important for you to take small steps and choose actions that are well within your capacity. It can be good to set goals for yourself one day at a time and move gradually to longer-term plans, for example a week at a time.

If you have a hard time coming up with ways to show yourself compassion, try to think of things you would advise your best friend to do in similar circumstances to your own. Can you show compassion in the same way?

Write down at least five things you know will do you good in the next days. Articulate them as precisely as possible, for instance going on a thirty-minute walk on a certain day at a certain time, setting aside fifteen minutes for relaxation, or calling a good friend and arranging to meet.

How do you want to praise yourself when you have done these things?

- ... By saying something kind about yourself?
- ... By buying yourself something nice?
- ... By doing something else?

KEEPING AN EMOTIONAL JOURNAL

It may be useful to you to keep a journal of your emotions in an effort to improve how you feel. Write the thoughts and feelings that play out inside you. Thoughts that are chaotic and disorganized may become clearer and more conscious when you manage to put them in words. This also permits you to express thoughts and feelings that you may not wish to share with others.

Some find it helps to write in the journal every day, while it suits others better to use it from time to time. It may be a relief to connect with your inner self and understand your feelings and thoughts better. When you have put an emotion into words on paper or on the computer screen, it is no longer as burdensome and doesn't have the same weight in your mind. If you aren't used to expressing yourself openly, this may be a bit difficult at first. You may start by writing mostly about where you're going and what you're doing. But that's quite alright. You've made a start, and with practice your writing will probably change and you will find yourself more able to connect with your emotions. You may have to write again and again about the same things. That's fine, and remember that it takes practice...

KEEPING A DIARY OF GRATITUDE

When your spouse is gone, it can be good to reminisce about what you are grateful for in the relationship. This diary allows you to thank your spouse for the love, intimacy, joy, warmth, and all the good times you shared. Here you can express your thanks for everything your spouse taught you. You can say thanks for all the little details and for having had this special person as a partner.

In your gratitude diary, you can also write your thoughts and feelings about being alive yourself and express your thanks for each new day.

A MINDFUL WALK IN NATURE

Give yourself a half-hour or an hour to go out for a walk. While you are walking, pay attention to what you see: the trees, the sky, nature, the ocean waves if you're by the sea. Alternatively, if you're in an entirely man-made environment, consider how it appears to you. Notice the sounds in your environment and whether you can smell the earth, the ocean, or something else. Consider how you walk, how heel and sole touch the ground by turns, whether you swing your arms. Move your arms in time with your legs. Notice how you breathe. Pay attention to all of this, how you swing your arms and legs, how you breathe, what you see and hear. Allow yourself to stop and look at a twig on a tree or pick up a pebble and roll it about in your fingers. Stand for a while with both feet planted evenly on the ground and take a deep breath. Feel the outside air in your lungs. Hold it in for a moment, then breathe out. Do this three times. Notice how you feel where you are standing out in the elements. Feel yourself to be a part of nature. Then keep walking and continue to pay attention to small things. If thoughts or worries from daily life creep up on you, observe that you have started to think. Let the thoughts that come to you fly by like birds in the sky.

LOOKING TO THE FUTURE – THE NEW ME

This assignment is meant for when you have moved forward in your grieving process. Consider yourself in your new circumstances. The purpose of this exercise is to stimulate creative thinking and encourage you to do ordinary things in unusual ways. Examine your immediate environment, the kitchen, living room, bedroom, the space you spend most of your time in. This space often reveals much about our inner lives. Is it messy, with stacks of paper here and there, unopened bills, closets full of clothes you never wear? It is often possible to make various changes at little expense. Go through the closets, buy a colorful poster, pull family photos out of albums and give them new life on the walls, buy new cushions or curtains or a potted plant for the living room. Making such changes can have a major impact on how you feel, stimulate the mind and be a tangible indication that life goes on in new ways. This can help you reevaluate things and take charge on your own terms.

Do something new every day. Do everyday things in unusual ways. Hold your coffee cup in the other hand, take a cold shower, drive a different way to work than usual, do something in a new way every single day.

Think about your health. Eat something healthy every day, try to get good rest at night, go to the gym, take walks, do yoga, take a dance course, play golf, listen to good music, and don't forget that laughter is the best medicine.

Find a new hobby. Look for courses that might interest you. Italian, belly dancing, fly tying, painting, creative writing. Find something that sparks your interest.

Make old dreams come true. Do you have something tucked away in the back of your mind that you've always wanted to do but never tried? Isn't it time to clear the dust off your old dreams? What were your dreams back in the day? Have you yet to make good on some of them? What are your dreams now?

Find an adventure. Remember that you have only this life. You didn't choose this situation, but you decide what comes next. Life is an adventure. You are allowed to have fun even though you are still grieving. You can still have plenty of fun even though you're alone. Think outside the box and allow yourself to dare to live.

Good luck!

BIBLIOGRAPHY

Abrahamowitz, F. 1999. **Det handler om mennesker. [It's about Human Beings.]** Copenhagen: Gyldendal.

Árnason, V. 1993. **Siðfræði lífs og dauða. [The Ethics of Life and Death.]** Reykjavík: Háskólaútgáfan.

Aron, E. N. 2013. **The Highly Sensitive Person.** (e-book). USA: Carol Publishing Group.

Azari, N.P., Janpeter, N., Wunderlich, G., et al. 2001. "Neural Correlates of Religious Experience." **European Journal of Neuroscience** 13: 1649-1652.

Benson, H. 2001. "Mind-Body Pioneer." (e-book). **Psychology Today** 3: 56-60.

Bergin, A.E. 1980. "Psychotherapy and religious values." **Journal of Consulting and Clinical Psychology** 48 (1): 95-105.

Brown, B. 2010. **The Gifts of Imperfection.** (e-book). USA: Brené Brown.

Brown, B. 2012. **Daring Greatly.** (e-book). USA: Gotham Books.

Buckman, R. 1988. **I Don't Know What to Say.** London: Papermac.

Burkeman, O. 2012. **The Antidote.** (e-book). London: Canongate.

Böhle, S. 2002. **Kroppens skjulte sprog. [The Body's Hidden Language.]** Copenhagen: Aschehoug Dansk Forlag A/S.

Cameron, J. 2000. **The Right to Write.** London: Macmillan.

Carlsson, K., Herrlin, B., and Olsson, A. 1994. **Tvillingar. [Twins.]** Stockholm: Bonnier Utbildning AB.

Carnelley, K., Wortman, C., Bolger, N., and Burke, C. 2006. "The time course of grief reactions to spousal loss: Evidence from a national probability sample." **Journal of Personality and Social Psychology** 91: 476-492.

Chopra, D., and Simon, D. 2004. **The Seven Spiritual Laws of Yoga.** New Jersey: John Wiley & Sons.

Chopra, D., and Tanzi R.E, 2012. **Super Brain.** (e-book) London: Rider.

Coelho, P. 2002. **Manual of the Warrior of Light.** London: HarperCollins Publishers.

Cope, S. 1999. **Yoga and the Quest for the True Self.** New York: Bantam Books.

Desikachar, T.K.V. 1995. **The Heart of Yoga.** Vermont: Inner Traditions International.

Dyregrov, A. 1993. **Beredskapsplan för skolan. [Contingency Planning for Schools.]** Stockholm: Rädda Barnen.

Dyregrov, A. 1994. **Att ta avsked. [Saying Goodbye.]** Stockholm: Rädda Barnen.

Dyregrov, A. 2006. "Komplisert sorg: teori og behandling." ["Complicated grief: theory and treatment."] **Tidsskrift for Norsk Psykologforening [Journal of the Norwegian Association of Psychologists]** 43: 779-786.

Dyregrov, A. 2010a. Barn og traumer. [Children and Trauma.] Bergen: Fagbokforlaget.

Dyregrov, A. 2010b. **Sorg hos barn. [The Grieving Child.]** Bergen: Fagbokforlaget.

Emmons, R.A. 2013. **Gratitude Works.** (e-book). USA: Robert A. Emmons.

Eriksson, E.H. 2000. **Den fullbordade livscykeln. [The Completed Life Cycle,]** Stockholm: Natur och Kultur.

Eydal, G. 2001. **Tvíburar. [Twins.]** Reykjavík: Uppeldi ehf.

Frankl, V.E. 1996. **Man's Search for Meaning.** Reykjavík: Háskólaútgáfan.

Gach, M.R. and Marco, C. 1981. **Acu-Yoga.** Tokyo: Japan Publications, Inc.

Germer, C.K. 2009. **The Mindful Path to Self-Compassion.** New York: The Guilford Press.

Ginsburg, G.D. 1997. **Widow to Widow.** Cambridge: Da Capo Press.

Goldberg, N. 1986. **Writing Down the Bones.** Boston: Shambhala.

Guðmundsdóttir, Á.E. 2005. **Mót hækkandi sól. [Toward the Rising Sun.]** Reykjavík: Salka.

Hendricks, G. 1995. **Conscious Breathing.** New York: Bantam Books.

Hoblitzelle, O.A. 2010. **Ten Thousand Joys and Ten Thousand Sorrows.** New York: Jeremy P. Tarcher/Penguin.

Hjálmarsson, S. 1973. **Eins konar þögn. [A Kind of Silence.]** Reykjavík: Hliðskjálf.

Holmes, T.H., and Rahe, R.H. 1967. "The Social Readjustment Rating Scale." **Journal of Psychosomatic Research** 11 (2): 213–8.

Horsley, G. and Horsley, H. **Spouse Loss.** (e-book). 2013. USA: Open to Hope Foundation and the authors.

Hurlimann-Lindseth, Ingvild. 2013. **Jeg skal fölge deg helt frem. [I Will Follow You All the Way.]** Oslo: Kagge Forlag A S.

Huxley, A. 1983. **Brave New World.** Harlow: Longman House.

Ingolfs, A., Eydal, G., and Bolladóttir, J.H. 2012 **Makalaust líf. [Life Without a Spouse.]** Reykjavík: Sögur- útgáfa.

Jörgensen, E. 2009. **Vi ses i morgen. [See You Tomorrow.]** Copenhagen: Rosinante.

Kirsta A. 1986. **Allt um streitu. [All About Stress.]** Reykjavík: Skjaldborg.

Klingberg, H., Jr. 2001. **When Life Calls Out to Us.** New York: Doubleday.

Kosmininsky, P. 2007. **Getting Back to Life When Grief Won't Heal.** New York: McGraw-Hill.

Kübler-Ross, E. 1986. **Death.** New York: A Touchstone Book.

Kübler-Ross, E. 1997. **The Wheel of Life.** New York: Simon & Schuster.

Kübler-Ross, E., and Kessler, D. 2012. **Life Lessons.** (e-book). New York: Scribner.

Laporte, D. 2012. **The Fire Starter Sessions.** (e-book). USA: Danielle Laporte, Inc.

Lasater, J. 2000. **Living Your Yoga.** California: Rodmell Press.

Laxness, H. 2002. **World Light.** Trans. Magnus Magnusson. New York: Vintage International.

Levang, E. 1998. **When Men Grieve.** Minneapolis: Fairview Press.

McGraw, P.C. 2001. **Livsstrategier. [Life Strategies.]** Copenhagen: Borgens Bogklub.

McGuinnes, M. 2012. **Resilience.** (e-book): Lateral Action Books

Miller, R. 2005. **Yoga Nidra – The Meditative Heart of Yoga.** Colorado: Sounds True.

Neff, K. 2011. **Self-Compassion.** (e-book). HarperCollins.

Oestrich, I.H. 2003. **Selvværd og Nye Færdigheder. [Self-Esteem and New Skills.]** Copenhagen: Psykologisk Forlag.

Oestrich, I.H., and Johansen F. 2005. **Kognitiv Coaching. [Cognitive Coaching.]** Copenhagen: Dansk Psykologisk Forlag.

Pálsson, S. 1998. **Börn og sorg. [Children and Grief.]** Reykjavík: Skálholtsútgáfan.

Pausch, R. 2008. **The Last Lecture.** London: Hodder & Stoughton.

Radha, S.S. 1989. **Hatha Yoga.** Boston: Shambhala.

Rasmussen, C., 2013. **Second Firsts.** (e-book). New York: Hay House.

Saraswati, S.S., 2003. **Yoga Nidra.** Munger, Bihar, India: Yoga Publications Trust.

Schiffmann, E. 1996. **The Spirit and Practice of Moving Into Stillness.** New York: Pocket Books.

Sigurbjörnsson, K. (ed.). 2006. **Bænabókin. [The Prayer Book.]** Reykjavík: Skálholtsútgáfan.

Silverman, P.R. 2004. **Widow to Widow.** New York: Brunner-Routledge.

Skúlason, B. 2001. **Sorg. [Grief.]** Reykjavík: Bragi Skúlason.

Steinþórsdóttir, Á., and Eydal, G. 1995. **Barnasálfræði. [Child Psychology.]** Reykjavík: Mál og menning.

Steinþórsdóttir, Á., and Eydal, G. 2003. **Í blóma lífsins. [In the Prime of Life.]** Reykjavík: Almenna bókafélagið.

Steinþórsdóttir, Á., and Eydal, G. 2007. **Ást í blíðu og stríðu. [Love through Thick and Thin.]** Reykjavík: Mál og menning.

Steinþórsdóttir, Á., and Eydal, G. 2010. **Sálfræði einkalífsins. [The Psychology of Private Life.]** Reykjavík: Sögur útgáfa.

Stephens, S. 2010. **The Effortless Sleep Method.** (e-book). UK: self-published.

Stroebe, M., Stroebe, W., and Schut, H. 2001. "Gender differences in adjustment to bereavement: An empirical and theoretical review." **Review of General Psychology** 5(1): 62-83.

Tolle, E. 2003. **Lev i Nuets Kraft. [Life in the Power of the Moment.]** Copenhagen: Borgens Bogklub.

Toohey, P. 2011. **Boredom.** London: Yale University Press

Wallace, W. 1998. **Living Again.** Kansas: Addax Publishing Group.

Worden, J.W. 1996. **Children and Grief.** New York: Guildford Press.

Worden, J.W. 2002. **Grief Counseling and Grief Therapy.** New York: Springer Publishing Company.

Þorsteinsdóttir, J.L. 2004. **Mig mun ekkert bresta. [I Shall Not Want.]** Reykjavík, Skálholtshútgáfan.

Columbia University of Social Work. What Is Complicated Grief? Viewed 15 October 2013.

http://www.complicatedgrief.org/bereavement

Elizabeth Harper Neeld – Grief Expert. Do Men Grieve Differently from Women? Viewed 15 October 2013.

http://www.connect.legacy.com/inspire/elizabeth-harper-neeld-grief

Griefspeaks. Men and Grief. Viewed 15 October 2013.

http://www.griefspeaks.com/id38.html

Mayo Clinic. Complicated Grief. Viewed 15 October 2013.

http://www.mayoclinic.org/diseases-conditions/complicated-grief/basics/causes/con-20032765

What to do When the Police Leave: A Guide to the First Days of Traumatic Loss, by Bill Jenkins. Men and Women in Grief. Viewed 15 October 2013. http://www.willsworld.com/men&women.htm

www.losingaspouse.com

FORGET-ME-NOT IN A FEW LANGUAGES

Chinese: 勿忘草属 *(wùwàngcâo shû)*

French: *ne m'oubliez pas*

German: *Vergissmeinnicht*

Icelandic: *Gleym-mér-ei*

Danish: *Markforglemmigej*

Norwegian: *Minneblom*

Swedish: *Förgätmigej*

Finnish: *Lemmikki*

Polish: *Niezapominajka*

Spanish: *no-me-olvides*

TWO STORIES ON THE ORIGINS OF THE FLOWER FORGET-ME-NOT

In a German legend, God was naming all the plants when a tiny unnamed one cried out, "Forget-me-not, O Lord!" God replied, "That shall be your name." Another legend tells that when the Creator thought he had finished giving the flowers their colours, he heard one whisper "Forget me not!" There was nothing left but a very small amount of blue, but the forget-me-not was delighted to wear such a light blue shade.

In 15th-century Germany, it was supposed that the wearers of the flower would not be forgotten by their lovers. Legend has it that in medieval times, a knight and his lady were walking along the side of a river. He picked a posy of flowers, but because of the weight of his armour he fell into the river. As he was drowning he threw the posy to his loved one and shouted "forget me not." It was often worn by ladies as a sign of faithfulness and enduring love.

(from Wikipedia, "Forget-me-not," retrieved 13 December 2013.)

Printed in Great Britain
by Amazon.co.uk, Ltd.,
Marston Gate.